Those Were the Days

Peter Stursberg with his dog, Taku, in 1936. (*Courtesy Peter Stursberg*)

Those Were the Days
Victoria in the 1930s

by
Peter Stursberg

Horsdal & Schubart

Horsdal & Schubart Publishers Ltd.
Victoria, B. C., Canada

Cover painting of the Empress Hotel, Victoria, B. C., by A.C. Leighton, courtesy of Canadian Pacific Limited; with special thanks to Nancy Williatte-Battet, Archives Assistant, Montreal, Quebec.

Printed and bound in Canada by Kromar Printing, Winnipeg, Manitoba

Canadian Cataloguing in Publication Data

Stursberg, Peter, 1913 -
Those were the days

    Originally published: Toronto : P. Martin Associates, 1969.
    ISBN 0-920663-23-0

    1. Stursberg, Peter, 1913   2. Nicholas, Benny
3. Journalists — Canada — Biography.   4. Victoria (B. C.) — Social life and customs.
I. Title.
PN4913.S8A3 1993   070.92   C93-091719-7

to Victoria and
Vancouver Island
in fond remembrance

INTRODUCTION to the SECOND EDITION

I am delighted that *Those Were The Days*, my memoirs of the 1930s, should be reprinted, as they are an account of what life was like, at least for a young man, in Victoria and on Vancouver Island in those days before the Second World War. They were a time of fading elegance, of tea parties and Saturday night dances at the Empress Hotel, and of a declining elite, not so much a British elite in this "little bit of Olde England", as the publicity bureau called it, but an Empire elite. There was the Great Depression, and while it was not as severe as in the rest of the country, it did affect the lotus eaters. One of the relief camps, the concentration camps for the single unemployed, was in the bush at Jordan River. Then, the clamorous world events, the rise of Fascism, the threat of war, did reach this sceptred outpost on the Pacific coast, but the worst news for Victoria's elite was the abdication. Edward VIII had let the side down. It was the end of an era, and the war only confirmed it.

Although I wrote this book in the 1960s, I tried to look at the times as if I were still a young and rather radical reporter. I was a self-declared socialist. Was it Beaverbrook who said that a young man who was not a socialist had no heart but who remained a socialist in middle age had no head? At any rate, I seemed to have been only too successful. That was the trouble. I faithfully copied the leftist lexicon and described the Chinese Customs Service and the Chinese Postal Service, for which my father worked, as "Imperialist rackets" and that caused him a great deal of anguish.

I had to apologise; in the letter that was published in the province's main newspapers in December 1969, I said:

"According to my father, 'both the former Chinese Customs Service and the Chinese Postal Service enjoyed the confidence and respect of the public, Chinese and foreign alike, that they served.' 'Any person,' he says, 'Who was served by that institution, [the Chinese Postal Service] in the days before China became split in two, will testify to its integrity and efficiency.'

"My father and other foreign employees of the Chinese Postal Service felt it an honor to have served in that service and to have shared in training its Chinese personnel, so that upon their final departure they left behind them an organization of which they could be justly proud. I wish to express my apologies to my father and others who served in the former Chinese Postal Service."

In retrospect, I must say that I was very insensitive and I regret any distress that I caused my father; I could have been less harsh in my criticism of Imperialist policy in China, and still have remained true to my left-wing views. While a Chinese government ostensibly ruled China, the treaty ports and concessions meant that the British and other westerners had all the advantages of a colony without it actually being a colony. My father was really a colonial civil servant, a very honourable profession. *Mea culpa.*

I was also criticized for revealing that B. C. "Benny" Nicholas, the beloved editor of the *Victoria Daily Times,* was an alcoholic and probably drank himself to death. This time it was said that I had overstepped the bounds of decency, that Benny was a saint and that his sins should not have been made public, which I had done. No one had a greater respect or love for the editor than I did — after all, he had hauled me out of the slough of despond that was unemployment. I thought that he was a warm and wonderful person but, unfortunately, no one is perfect; I felt that I could not describe him fully without mentioning his failures, which he had done his best to overcome. It was part of the human condition.

The 1930s were a period of transition, even for Victoria. The newspapers had not become big business, and while the *Times* was owned by the Spencers of the Spencer Department Store, it received subsidies from the Liberal Party. And a great editor such as Benny Nicholas could run a newspaper and was more important than the publisher or owner. We, reporters, were miserably paid and longed for a union, but sadly, those of us who fought for and finally joined the American Newspaper Guild were to become disenchanted with the organization.

Almost every house had a radio set, but wireless, as it was called, had not yet challenged the newspapers as a news medium. Talking pictures seemed to have sounded the death knell of the stage. No touring company had visited Victoria in years. A leader of the local thespians, Major Bullock-Webster, asserted that the tradition of live theatre would have to be carried on by amateur groups like the Beaux Arts or the Little Theatre.

It was the glorious "swing time", the time of the big bands, and Victoria had its own big bands; one led by Billy Tickle played in the ballroom of the Empress Hotel at the Saturday night dances. Billy Tickle was transformed in the afternoons into William Tickle and his string ensemble, playing for the ladies having tea in the flower-filled hotel lobby.

The Spanish Civil War was the Vietnam of the period, and had a great emotional impact; people argued angrily about it and families split over it. Lionel Backler, a reporter and friend on the *Times*, joined the International Brigades and was killed. A Socialist Party was formed with the extraordinary name of Cooperative Commonwealth Federation (CCF) and almost immediately became the official opposition in the B. C. Legislature; amoeba-like, it kept breaking up but growing. A tweedy gent from up-island got himself elected on the tenets of the Oxford Group, later known as Moral Rearmament. Near us were a couple of British Israelites, who found mysterious messages in the measurements of the pyramids. Technocracy flourished, and I saw recently an old lady, like a ghost from the past, carrying a technocracy sign at an environmentalist demonstration!

Those Were The Days, and they are lost and gone. A lost Aileen. A lost youth. But there are reminders. Beacon Hill Park for one, and Butchart Gardens: if anything, they are more beautiful. The inner harbour has much the same appearance. On one side, the monumental pile of the Parliament Buildings that "Pinkie" McKelvie, a fervid colonial separatist, would have converted into a casino, and in the centre, that cynosure, the Empress Hotel, still the symbol and hallmark of Victoria.

Peter Stursberg, June 1993

1

Getting a job was the greatest achievement bar none in the days of my youth. I know because I knocked on doors and answered ads and filled in forms for two years, only to be told there was nothing, nothing, nothing, although that wasn't always the reply. "Leave your name and we'll let you know" — and like a goof, you became hopeful although you knew there was no hope, there was nothing. A job meant everything in the thirties: it was an escape from the dreariness of the depression, and a chance to live it up after all the aching dullness of nothing to do, nowhere to go. Cyril Lee's description of life in a relief camp — an indefinite prison sentence — was a good description of unemployment; even outside the camp, life was like a prison sentence.

I had got what I wanted by camping on the doorstep of Benny Nicholas, called the greatest small town editor in Canada by many a newspaperman, "the Canadian William Allan White", the "most unforgettable character" he had ever met by Bruce Hutchison — as for me, I just figured he was the greatest guy in the world *period*. I became a reporter on the *Victoria Daily Times* and kicked the gray chicken shit of unemployment off my boots. All my ganglions were twitching as I caught up with what I had missed in the years without work, the years without money, the years without.

My circle of friends now included some of the society babes who belonged to the Beaux Arts, which was the equivalent of the Junior League in Victoria, only the Beaux Arts was supposed to be more cultural and put on plays and concerts as well as dances. Not only were these babes better lookers and better dressers than the country girls at the Anglican Young People's Association (AYPA) meetings in Royal Oak, where we lived, but they had a lot more oomph, if you know what I mean. One of them was Aileen which wasn't her real name, but then she wasn't always the same girl, and in looking back through the haze of time, she may have been more a symbol or a dream. Instead of gawking at the great wooden mansions in Rockland like a beggar at the gate, I had been in these homes of the well-established wealthy, the mining and lumber millionaires — the bootleggers and newer rich were building houses in the Uplands which was just opening up then.

Above all, there was the clattering excitement of the *Times'* news room, the sense of urgency there, the smell of hot news, which was the smell of the cleaning fluid that the janitor used. I had a feeling that I was at the centre of things, and I was — this was in the days before broadcasting had taken over, although radio was already breathing down our necks with eyewitness accounts of the Moose River Mine disaster and the Hindenburg crash. A newspaper was a newspaper was a newspaper, as Gertrude Stein might have said. And there were the characters in the news room: Archie Wills, the news editor; Bill Henderson, the telegraph editor; and the reporters, especially Lionel Backler, whom I couldn't fail to notice because he was six feet, seven inches tall and had a leonine head with a great mane of brown hair.

Lionel was the office radical and he fascinated and shocked me. I was indignant when he attacked my hero, Ben Nicholas (who was such a loveable guy — the Great Humanitarian I would have called him) as an "economic royalist", which was about the worst thing you could say of anyone, short of calling him a "fascist hyena". There was not a grain of gratitude in Lionel, for the editor was helping him to work his way through college by giving him a summer job on the *Times*.

"Benny's a Liberal hack," Lionel would go on, "and what I can't stand is the way he patronizes me."

However, his antipathy had no effect on the editor, who maintained his sunny avuncular disposition at all times, although he did become irritated with Lionel's more extreme utterances and his unquestioning support for the Bolsheviks. Actually, Benny, who was a roly-poly Mister Five-by-Five, liked tall young men, and that was why he put up with so much nonsense, as he called it, from Lionel.

Nothing was sacred to this son of an Engineer-Captain in the Royal Navy, who had a contemptuous disregard for everything that the paper stood for and for almost everyone in the newsroom. He referred to Bruce Hutchison, who was writing a column for the *Times* then and was considered to be liberal if not socialist in his views, as the "Junker of Saanich", which was an amusing and apt dig — and even I, in my political naivety, realized this — since Bruce had a comfortable country home in Saanich where he did most of his work and he preached the most orthodox financial opinions and even then was crying out against the dangers of government spending and inflation.

There was a certain intellectual arrogance about Lionel, and he must have been a trial to Benny and Archie Wills, but he dazzled me; he had the answers to so many of the questions that I was asking. Beside him, my other friends seemed ignorant and unaware, even though such people as Cyril Lee and his brother Gordon had had experiences which Backler had not, and no doubt, would have liked to have. The Lee boys had been in a relief camp at Jordan River, while Lionel had been wallowing in bourgeois ease (as he would have put it) at the University of British Columbia in Vancouver. Of course, that didn't mean to say that Cyril and Gordon hadn't been affected by the camp; they had — but they didn't have Lionel's political faith, his certainty that he had found salvation. They were still lost.

As for the rest of the AYPA crowd at Royal Oak, once I began to work, they faded away like the old soldiers in the veterans' clubs, and I didn't see them any more. In retrospect, I must say that I appear to have been a social climber, a young man on the make. Yet, what is wrong with that? Who isn't a social climber? It's part of the human struggle, of evolution or the rat race or whatever you want to call it. It was just more violent in the thirties. We were in a greater hurry then because we had started late and had farther to climb, and it was too bad if friends were left behind, but *c'est la vie*. My progress had been almost straight up, as there was a tremendous gap between the unemployed and the employed; they were the only classes in the great depression, the working class and the non-working class, and they were so far apart, they might have been different nations in the same country.

Then, I should explain that I came from a rather isolated community, the country folk on the city's edge, although I wasn't a country boy myself, and it was entirely fortuitous that I should have been scrabbling around in the chicken shit before I got a job on the *Times*.

1930-1934

2

What got me down about those application forms were the questions: where were you born and what experience do you have? How the hell could I have had any experience when I had just finished two years of an arts and science course at McGill University with a couple of sups, which would never be taken now that I had had to quit college. It was the old runaround: you couldn't get a job without experience and you couldn't get experience without a job. And then, what difference did it make where I was born? Not that I was ashamed of my birthplace, which was Chefoo, China, although it had proved to be a bloody nuisance, especially when crossing the border. You should have seen the look of bemusement on the faces of the immigration officials. It was as if I had been born in Hades-on-the-Styx. "Would you mind waiting a moment, sir," and a lot more stupid questions before I could go on.

By a curious coincidence, my best pal at McGill, Shep McMurtry, who is still a close friend, was also born in China (his father, Dr. S. O. McMurtry, was a medical missionary). He got tired of getting the business over this accident of birth and hit on the fiendishly clever idea of answering "Lachine" whenever he was asked where he was born. "Lachine", and if the dumb Yank wanted to know where that was, he would reply that Lachine was a suburb of Montreal. No further fuss — and he hadn't committed any perjury.

My father was not a missionary; he was in the Chinese postal service when it was run by foreigners and was a classical example of old-fashioned imperialism. I should explain that the Chinese postal service grew out of the Chinese customs service which the British set up originally to collect the indemnity levied on China for losing the infamous Opium War. It was really the greatest racket. Since the British were in cahoots with the French in the despoliation of China, the French were given the postal service, while the British retained the lucrative customs service. So, there was always a French chief of the Chinese postal service, as there was always a British head of the Chinese customs service (Sir Robert Hart was the most famous). Shortly after I was born in August, 1913, my father was transferred to Peking where he became secretary to M. Theophile Piry, the French director general of the postal service.* (Significantly enough, French was not one of the working languages; they were English and Chinese.)

The time in China that I remember best was the early twenties when my father was postal commissioner of Honan Province, and we lived in a great new house which had wide verandahs and separate servants' quarters and stables and a two-and-a-half acre garden which included a tennis court; the assistant commissioner's house was next door, and it was slightly less grand and had a garden half the size of ours. This was the postal commissioner's compound, and the whole of it was surrounded by a high brick wall; it was across a dirt road from the American missionaries' compound and a mile away from the old walled city of Kaifeng, the capital of Honan and one-time capital of China (during the Sung dynasty).

It was a lordly life all right (we had eleven servants to run the great house and garden), and although my father enjoyed it, he knew it couldn't last; he was never taken in by Kipling and all the crap about the white man's burden, as so many old China hands were. On one of his furloughs home, he bought a bungalow with seven acres of property on Vancouver Island: it was to be a haven from China. When Chiang Kai-shek and the nationalists began throwing out the Christian missionaries, my father figured it was time to go — not that he had any regard for the missionaries, but he was being insulted and called a foreign devil to his face, and he knew that the good old days of Empire were gone. That was in 1927.

He had no difficulty in finding employment on his return to Canada. This was during the pre-depression boom, and we moved to Montreal where he became development officer for a large chemical combine. For three or four years he proposed new projects for this big business, some of which were undertaken. However, when the crash came, there was no more expansion but rather contraction; the last person needed was a development officer, and in the fall of 1931, my father was let out. I remember that dismal day: my mother wept and my father looked embarrassed as he always did at any display of emotion, and I felt cold and empty and very much alone. It was a familiar little tragedy that year when the economy was shutting down and thousands were laid off in Montreal alone. Goddamit, there were more victims of the depression than casualties in the war, but people seem to have forgotten that now.

For a time, my father tried to sell insurance, which was the purgatory that most men of his age and experience suffered at that time; it was a

*The first man to hold the office. He was succeeded in 1915 by M. H. Picard Destelan, who held the office of co-director general jointly with a Chinese colleague. In this way the natives were trained to take over the service.

hopeless business, and he loathed calling on people who didn't want to see him. It was all so undignified, especially for an old China hand, and in the summer of 1932, he decided to escape from Montreal, which was hard hit, and where there were soup kitchens and suicides and a heavy atmosphere of failure, to Vancouver Island and his small holding there. More than one quarter of Canadian workers were unemployed then,* more than twelve million in the United States, and revolution, not prosperity, was around the corner. He hitched a trailer to our box-shaped Chevrolet, and despite blowouts and accidents, reached the Pacific Coast after ten days of driving.

Our place was at the foot of Little Saanich Mountain, atop which was the white dome of the Dominion Observatory. It had been badly neglected — in fact, my father had almost forgotten about it — and it was overgrown with broom, but there was a small orchard and a hay field and a white-painted clapboard bungalow on a moss-covered rock. As a farm, it would not support the best farmer, but for someone like my father with a small income, it was a pine-scented haven, not from China and its raging nationalists, but from the great depression.

*According to DBS, the peak of unemployment came in 1933, with 646,000 out of work; this represented 26.5 percent of the total estimated wage earners of the time.

3

Let me reiterate: before employment, life was not "just a bowl of cherries", which always struck me as a pretty silly simile even for a pop song. To be frank, life was lousy, just plain dull and dreary. That is my memory of the great depression, which reached its depth in 1933, when the banks closed in the United States: the Canadian banks didn't close and they were to brag about this, but as Lionel said, they kept open by closing down Canadian industry. Capitalism was a real bust, and everybody said so, but this didn't make much difference to us in our island refuge. No one really suffered. No one starved — at least, no one I knew. There were soup kitchens and grocery handouts and relief camps. "Don't let the sucker die" — that was the new humanitarianism.

The worst was when it rained. It was bad enough when the sun shone, but when it rained the gray emptiness of everything made for an ache in your guts as you cleaned out the chicken house, half doubled up because the roof was so low, the water dripping down your neck through the cracks in the rotten shingles. We had a couple of hundred chickens, white Leghorns and Rhode Island Reds, but eggs were so cheap, they hardly paid for their feed. Chicken shit — it got on your boots and on your hands, and the dank stench of it, combined with the rain, the cold gray rain of the Pacific Coast, to turn the chicken shit world of ours into a slimy gumbo.

For a few weeks in the summer there was work to be had on the farms, picking berries, strawberries and cherries. At first, I wondered if I would ever make a buck, it took so long to fill a hallock, or basket, for which you got one or two cents, and then I wondered if I would survive, bent double or crawling in the dirt. What a cripes awful job! In the end, I earned a couple of bucks, which was about all you could make in a day without having ten hands like one of those Hindu dieties, and when you worked it out, this wasn't bad pay for the times. In any case, there was nothing else to do.

About the only social life there was for a young fellow like myself, who didn't have two nickels to rub together, was at the church — in the St. Michael's branch of the Anglican Young People's Association, to be specific. We lived in the sticks, although we were no more than seven miles from Victoria's gingerbread masterpiece of a city hall, but we were deep in the country then and divided from the city by the empty nothingness of the depression, although it is possible that life wasn't very different for a fellow without a job in the city.

St. Michael's Anglican Church was about halfway between us and Royal Oak on the West Saanich road, which was a branch of the main road to Victoria, the other branch being the East Saanich road. Royal Oak was at the juncture of the West and East roads and among its half-dozen buildings was the Saanich Municipal Hall. This was typical Pacific Northwest scenery, the hills covered with scrub oak trees, great cedars and hemlock, as well as balsam and pine, and everywhere the dogwood, its great white flowers adopted as the provincial emblem, and the exotic arbutus; we had an arbutus in front of our house and its habit of shedding its bark in summer used to annoy my father, who was a tidy gardener. Much of Saanich Peninsula was closely cultivated, and the church, which was at the top of a rise in the road, looked down on the black currant rows of the Mackinnon farm, and beyond to the sheep pastures of the old Metzger homestead and other farms hazily outlined in the blue distance. It was, as the Reverend Fred Comely observed on more than one occasion, like a view of the Surrey downs.

Mr. Comely was a short thickset man with a shock of white hair, who was closer to seventy than sixty and yet was a keen cricketer who played for the Cathedral team in the Victoria League. He was an Englishman, as most Anglican clergymen were, but had been on the Coast for some time and had been a missionary to the Indians up-island; Mrs. Comely was a tall, gaunt woman, almost a head taller than her husband, who looked the part of a missionary's wife. St. Michael's vicar had a comfortable and comforting appearance; he put on no airs and although he was well educated for the times, still spoke with the common accent of his youth. His sermons were short and simple and he never talked down from his pulpit. Despite his humble origin, Mr. Comely was a conservative and seldom mentioned unemployment or the depression. This pleased his congregation, who were mostly stump ranchers, but included some well-to-do retired folks who didn't want to be reminded of such gloomy things.

The Anglican Young People's Association, St. Michael's branch, met in the church hall, a frame and stucco building a step down the hill from the white clapboard church with its modest forward belfry. The vicarage, which was above the church, was a substantial wooden bungalow of the same design as so many of the older houses in Victoria that one wondered whether the same set of blueprints was used for all of them — the sun room was always in front and served as an entrance hall. The garden flourished under the ministrations of the Reverend Mr. Comely, who offended some of his parishioners, mostly the retired folk, by working in tattered overalls in full view of those passing on the road. His rose beds and well-cut lawn were separated by a wire fence from the weeds that surrounded the church.

Frank Doyle was the head of the AYPA for as long as I was a member; he was in his twenties, a heavily built man with a weather-reddened face, watery blue eyes and sandy hair and great hams of hands which were gnarled and rough. It was with these hands that he had cleared the Doyle place and built their house, so my mother and other mothers said, for Frank was greatly admired by all who attended St. Michael's. His father had been killed in a tragic accident, and Frank had to take on the responsibility of minding a family while still a schoolboy; it was a heavy burden and there was no one to share it.

When I saw Frank Doyle some three years later, after I had become a reporter, I hardly recognized him; he was bent over like some heavy beast of burden, which he had become in his desperate efforts to tear a farm out of the bush above the West Saanich road, an old man before his time.

Most of the AYPA meetings were taken up with playing party games, since Frank Doyle didn't approve of dancing, at least not the cheek-to-cheek kind; he might have gone for the old time dancing but we were too close to the city for that, and even though most of the kids were from the farms around, they scorned the agricultural hall "hops" to which their parents went. So there were charades, and truth or consequences, and a game called murder, which was played with the lights out to the delight of the company; as soon as the "murder" was committed, the lights were supposed to go on, but there was always a great deal of giggling and fumbling around with the switch, especially when Mary was the victim. She was the only girl to flaunt her breasts in a tight sweater, and she was the favourite choice of the "murderers". There were those who complained that the game was too realistic, but Mary never did. However, Frank Doyle got a ruling from Mr. Comely that the lights should not be put out in the church hall during an AYPA social; we could play murder with the lights on, but no one wanted to, and that ended that.

Still, the AYPA was the only fun to be had in those penniless times, and for that I was grateful. Just meeting other young people was a thrill, and I would go whistling down the West Saanich road in the cedar-scented dusk of summer, past the rich odours of Chew Dang's market garden and the Beaver Lake road on the left, where the Wards lived in a triangle-shaped house, a mad couple of British Israelites, constantly muttering incomprehensible prophecies; past the little lean-to where Miss Oades and her cousin Eulalie sold cigarettes and candies, and the old neglected orchard, and the ramshackle farmhouse, to Rev. Comely's rose garden and St. Michael's Church and church hall, and then it was just a few bounding steps up to the wooden stoop and inside.

4

It was plumb crazy, although it didn't seem so crazy then, that Gordon and Cyril Lee should have been in a relief camp. Of all the Royal Oak crowd, they were among the best off, or at least, their old man was well off. Their father, Charles Lee, was an old China hand like mine; he had recently retired from the Salt Gabelle,* and instead of returning to the old country, had settled on Vancouver Island and built a Georgian style house on the side of the hill near St. Michael's Church. He was a stiff, rather formal figure with a beard and the dry, sallow appearance of a person who had been too long in a hot climate. The old China hands were a closely knit community and Mr. Lee knew my father by his nickname.

"Can you imagine it, Stussie," he said. "When we got here, what did we find but the two boys on relief — yes, in one of the bloody camps that Bennett put up for the single men, along with a most dreadful lot of unemployed and deadbeats."

"Good God," Mr. Lee continued as he picked his way around the edge of the velvet-smooth Peking rug in the long drawing room that stretched the length of his house, "and here we had sent them to Charterhouse."

His indignation was amusing, and I stifled a guffaw, but Gordon and Cyril didn't think it was funny. They resented the way their father talked about their experience in the relief camp, which they had now become half-proud of, just as the old sweats, swilling beer in the Canadian Legion clubs, were half-proud of the abominations they suffered during the war. We were having tea in the long drawing room which was full of Chinese ornaments, scrolls depicting fierce fat men or fierce folk tales, cloisonné and porcelain bowls of various shapes and sizes on carved blackwood stands, yellowing ivory carvings, a glass case full of snuff bottles and jade bric-a-brac, and silver vases and boxes, all embellished with the dragon design.

Afterwards, we sat chewing the rag in the boys' basement room, and Gordon grumbled in his hoarse voice that always sounded so confiden-

*A copy of the Indian organization, which controlled and taxed the production of salt.

tial that the old man was full of hot air, that there were some bums in the relief camp but mostly good guys who just couldn't find work and had to eat.

But, how come they were in a relief camp?

Well, the explanation was that when they finished school, they hadn't liked working for their father in Shanghai and had persuaded him to send them to Vancouver Island, where they knew he planned to retire. When they arrived in Victoria in 1930, it was easy to get a job, and both of them worked on a road crew surveying a route up-island. They had a great time, blazing a trail through the forests of cedar and fir, the great sea of trees that rolled majestically up to the horizon and merged there in the blue distance with the sea itself. Only the survey job didn't last for long and then there was no work to be had, and the boys, who had argued their father into paying their way to Vancouver Island, were too proud to tell him that they were unemployed now and flat broke and needed a handout.

So, they applied for relief and were put in a camp at Jordan River, about forty miles from Victoria up the wild west coast of Vancouver Island. It was another camp among the many camps, the CCC camps in the United States, the concentration camps in Europe, the relief camps of Canada; the camps were part of the worldwide conspiracy to bury the youth of the times, to clear the single unemployed men off the streets of the towns and cities where they were an embarrassment with their tin-canning, as begging was called, and hide them, bury them, in the bush; out of sight, out of mind, and in the camps, they would be out of the view of the populace and off the conscience of humanity. At Jordan River, the camp was a collection of tar paper shacks in a clearing in the woods; it was so far away from anyone that the nearest habitation was the half-built house of a stump rancher some fifteen miles down the West Coast road, which was nothing but a dirt track that petered out just beyond the camp. The men worked on the road and were paid twenty cents a day, a slave labour rate, although it was no slave labour.

Most of the time, the men spent leaning on their spades, smoking and grumbling about how lousy life was. Aside from the miserable pay, there was no incentive to work, nothing ennobling about this labour; there was no equipment, just pick and shovels, and no desire, it seemed, on the part of anyone to do anything but scrabble around.

"Just digging a hole and filling it in again?"

"Yeah, that was about it."

Cyril rolled some makings expertly. The boys had converted the basement of the Lee's house into their own quarters: there was a long table on which they had their correspondence course books and papers (they were both taking courses in radio engineering), and some beat-up old chairs which were comfortable enough. You could always rest your feet on the table, which you couldn't do in the long drawing room upstairs — not bloody likely.

When Gordon and Cyril got out of the relief camp, as soon as their father arrived in Victoria, they couldn't get anything to do, which was hardly surprising as it was the depth of the depression, 1932 and all that. In the end their father put them to work on his property, which ran up the side of a hill. They were turning it into a terraced garden, with tier upon tier of flower beds, rose arbors, shrubberies, rockeries, fountains and pools, rising above the curve of the road; "the hanging gardens of Saanich", Dad called it, more in admiration than derision.

A couple of old Carthusians at Jordan River. Row, row, row, only it wasn't that kind of river, the river Jordan, pardon, Jordan River. Then, dig, dig, and don't dig. Green grow the rushes-oh! Ha, Ha! The chaps at the British Public School Boys Club in Victoria wouldn't have approved, but then the times were out of joint for everyone, there was no denying that, and the Old Boys and their club were caught in the whirlpool, they didn't escape, as I was to find out.

It was difficult to get the boys to talk about life in the relief camp, but when they did, their choice of expletives made it clear that it was a pretty depressing experience. Cyril said that it was what prison life must be like. You could get out all right — that was true enough. There was a truck going to Victoria every couple of days, and you could hitch a ride if you wanted. There was nothing to prevent you from taking off for town and staying there — nothing except money, and if you started tin-canning to eat, you'd soon be hustled back to camp.

They used to go to town about once a week, jouncing over the rough dirt road they weren't building, because, as Gordon said, they had to get away from the camp and "those godawful tar paper shacks" or they'd go mad. What really got the boys down was that there wasn't a chair in the camp — the government was that cheap — just the bunks and the benches and tables in the hut that was used as a mess hall. When they got to Victoria, they just hung around the streets; they couldn't afford to go to a movie very often, not on twenty cents a day, and they didn't know anyone and didn't want to know anyone.

Most of the men in the camp didn't come from the Island. A lot were from the prairies. They had ridden the rods to the Coast to escape the prairie winter, and some bastard had paid their way across to the Island, telling them that there was work to be had over there, but really just getting them out of Vancouver.

There was a friend of their father whom they had met when they had first come over and who had been kind to them. They never saw him after they were put in a relief camp because they didn't want to admit that they were down and out and they never let on to their parents what had happened.

"Until he arrived here, the old man thought that we still had that job up-island," Gordon said with a hoarse chuckle.

Cyril said that they longed to see this friend of their father because he used to give them a bang-up feed and had a very pretty daughter. However, it wasn't the feed that he dreamed about at camp, but sitting in the man's luxuriously comfortable arm chairs.

"Not the beautiful daughter?" I asked.

"Oh no," Cyril said, "that wouldn't have been at all realistic. It would have cost money to take her out, and we didn't have any."

Yes, money: it was the root of all our ills, of all our hopeless yearnings and our bitter frustrations in the thirties. What was it old Robinson said? He was the pensioner who lived next door to us in a wooden shack not much bigger than a packing case, which could be reached by a path through the pine trees at the bottom of our place. There was a stench about that shack like the stench in a Canadian Legion club or a beer parlour, only this was stronger and more yeasty, for old Robinson was engaged in making his own beer, as was almost everyone else in those days; his one room was stacked with bottles, the empties in one corner and the full ones in another. Home brew was the main drink during the depression, and it was either too yeasty or flat with a taste of rusty nails, so that a bottle of branded beer was a treat because it was so smooth to drink. Actually, old Robinson's beer was among the best, and Robinson helped my father with his brew, although we were bigger on cider because we had our small orchard and there was nothing to be done with the apples — you couldn't sell them, you couldn't even give them away — but mash them up in a borrowed machine and make a cider that was hard and dry, as long as it was not drunk too soon.

"A young fellow-me-lad like you," old Robinson said when I was sampling a bottle from his latest brew, "should have a five-dollar bill in his pocket so he can show his girl a good time."

It was the amount which stuck in my mind. Five bucks — but it was a lot of money in the thirties, five lousy simoleans, it could buy you independence: at least, it could get you a ticket of leave or a brief parole from the dismal prison of the depression, where most of us wasted some of the best years of our lives.

5

My trouble was that I had tasted independence and life in the big city of Montreal before coming to Vancouver Island, and this made my discontent even greater. I hadn't driven out with the family in the old Chev as I had a summer job in Montreal, and when it ended, I worked my way across the continent on a CPR "Chink train", guarding Chinese who were travelling in bond to the Pacific Coast to catch a ship to China.

It was the first time that I had been on my own and I savoured every moment of it, especially the carefree feeling of not having to worry about Mum's waiting up or what Dad thought. It was bliss all right: the hot, sultry city streets of that summer had the promise of adventure, and there was the whispering wonder of Montreal at night: what was going on behind those glowing curtains? I hated to leave in September. There was no one I knew on the Coast, and the country life was not meant for a cosmopolitan such as I; I longed to go back to Montreal.

I wanted to return to McGill University, or I thought I did, and said so repeatedly to my parents, which distressed them more than somewhat, especially my father, who felt guilty about taking refuge in this backwoods where there was no possibility of my completing my education, as there was no university. Not that I was a very good student: I had a couple of sups and would have a rough time getting my year if I had been able to go back. No, it wasn't university or the science course (although I had visions of myself as a research chemist, dressed in white and working in a lab), that made me want to return, but the freedom of being on my own in Montreal, and the McGill rowing crew, and my old friend, Shep McMurtry, and the raffish life of the tourist bus drivers and spielers.

Come to think of it, I spent much of the summer at the rowing club which had an old, gray-painted, clapboard house at Valois on the Lakeshore, but the city was just over the horizon, shining bright, and its temptations were within easy commuter reach. In fact, I took the train to town every day, as I worked as a summer replacement in the purchasing department of Canadian Industries Limited, which had offices in the new Bell Telephone Building on Beaver Hall Hill. It was a rigorous life: we used to row at five o'clock in the morning on placid Lake St. Louis, then breakfast and off to work, and row again at six in the evening on our return from the city, so that we were ready to bed down early and there was no chance of monkey business, although there were the weekends.

Shep was in the same four as I (we were in the second four of the McGill eight), and we set some kind of an unbreakable record by turning over a coxless four. It was said to be impossible to do, since the long oars were supposed to provide a balance, but we did it. I figure that Shep and I, we both rowed on the stroke side, must have "caught crabs" at the same time, and whoosh, over the shell went, although I don't really remember what happened. We were just starting off with short chopping strokes when the next thing I knew we were in the water, looking very foolish, with the coach's "Gott-fur-doomers" rumbling across the lake.

We had a great coach in Urbain Molmans, a Belgian who was built like a barrel and had been a championship oarsman in his day; he was a slave driver but he did a remarkable job in whipping such unpromising material into shape. He had very little selection, as not many students could be persuaded to pay for the privilege of being "galley slaves" all summer. But he shouldn't have entered us in the Olympic Trials of 1932 at Port Dalhousie; I guess Molmans was just desperate. At any rate, we were outclassed and came in last in the eights, although there were only four entries. We drove to Port Dalhousie along Highway 2, the shell having gone ahead in a truck with Molmans sitting guard, and even though it was boiling hot on the Niagara Peninsula and our practises and races were swelteringly strenuous, we liked to go roller skating at a nearby roadhouse. Such was our condition.

That was at the end of July. The rowing was over after we had come in fourth out of four in the Olympic Trials, and so we quit the gray house at Valois on the Lakeshore, and I moved into a fraternity house on the fringe of the McGill campus. There was the usual kind of party to mark the end of the summer rowing, and in some trepidation, we visited a whorehouse off St. Denis Street. We left after a drink, which we figured was the least that was expected from us, but even then the ladies of the house, who seemed to be wearing fishnets for clothes, jeered at us as we hurried, hot-faced, out. It was the sort of party that is talked about for several weeks after, but is not really memorable.

I don't recall whether I got a room in Shep's fraternity, the Psi U, or the Zete house, or at the Dekes', but every fraternity was looking for summer lodgers, and this one, whatever it was, seemed to be the headquarters of the fellows who worked on the tourist buses. They were an odd mixture of college boys and young hoodlums, the spielers — the drivers were mostly respectable family men, although one or two would turn up at the fraternity house. As they were dressed alike in the gray uniforms of the bus line, it was difficult to tell the undergraduates from the hoods, especially since the students tended to imitate the young punks with whom they worked. It was never the other way around, and I wondered why this should be. What was that about the adulteration of money? Wasn't the same sort of thing happening to language? The vulgar tongue was much more virile and earthy, and beside it the academic accent sounded pedantic and precious.

One student spieler whom I knew had developed a tough Brooklyn accent of his own. He tended to speak out of a corner of his mouth and went out of his way to be ungrammatical. If he missed a double negative, he would go back to pick it up. "He's done nuttin' ", he would say and correct himself, "He ain't done nuttin' ". The same was true of a couple of others, whose repertoire of obscenities and profanities was not extensive but was in constant use.

Almost every night there was a poker game in one of the bedrooms, the boys ranged around a table, cigarettes drooping from their lips, their shirts open or off, as it was dripping hot that August in Montreal. Empty beer bottles littered the floor, and there was usually a dozen full bottles being kept cool in the bathtub down the hall. One of the students would have his family car, and we would drive out to a summer dance hall in Lachine, where they didn't have taxi dancers at ten cents a dance but the girls came on their own, and you could figure on a pickup. Zowie — but the girls came in pairs and I usually got the chaperone and not the beauty. Then, there were the weekends amid the delights of Como on the Lake of Two Mountains, where the McMurtrys had a summer place; actually, Swiss ancestors of Shep's on the Shepherd side of his family had named Como after the Swiss Como, and old Captain Shepherd had run the river boats from Montreal past Como and Hudson and Hudson Heights up to Ottawa.

It was all over too soon, and I had to board the colonist car of the Chink train in the CPR Windsor Station. The full time guard was a toothless old bastard who gave me the worst shift, from 12:00 midnight to 8:00 in the morning; when I fell asleep during one such shift he prodded me awake and, I learned later, put in a bad report on me. Most of the Chinese we were supposed to guard had paid their way and were certainly not going to jump the train, but there was one deportee. This was September, 1932, the depth of the depression, and there were many riding the rods, or riding behind the tenders of the steam engines or between the railway cars. I would see them in the railway yards, standing around waiting for the train to start, as the passengers did on the station platform; sometimes a cop would appear and they would scatter, but they were back almost before he was out of sight. Not all rode the rods: when I was standing on the steps as we pulled out of a whistle stop in the Rockies, a couple of burly men in knee britches and windbreakers shoved me aside and entered the baggage car.

6

As I have said more than once, but it bears repeating, it's the dreariness of life that's my chief memory of the depression, the aching dullness of nothing to do. I tried desperately to get a job, going vainly from one employment office to another, meanwhile scrounging odd jobs like fruit picking whenever I could.

By the end of 1933, most of us had given up looking for work — what was the point of it when there was none, and we were becoming bums, but without any hallelujah chorus, thank you. I don't remember who it was who first proposed working in the woods on our own. Maybe it was Sunny Gilroy, whom we had got to know although he lived in town; he had heard about a stand of timber near Prospect Lake where the farmer wanted little or no stumpage. This was second growth but of a good size. Hell no — we wouldn't be cutting for the sawmills in Victoria but for stove wood, and that was one thing that hadn't gone down in price — it still brought between four and six dollars a cord, delivered.

Beside Sunny, my brother Richard, and I and a fellow called Murphy were in on the deal. Perhaps it was Murphy, who lived in a run-down area named Happy Valley, who knew about the timber stand. At any rate, we were able to borrow the necessary equipment, the single-bladed axes, the two-man crosscut saw with its inch-deep teeth, the iron wedges and sledge hammer for splitting the logs, and even a peavey, the spiked lever used for moving lumber.

It was hard work, swinging the axe on its long shaft, chipping out the undercut in great yellow chunks, but it was man's work, and nothing demeaning like scrabbling around on your hands and knees picking strawberries or cleaning out the chicken houses. There was a technique to sending the crosscut saw whistling through the wood, spilling a cone of sawdust; it was tough to acquire, but once you got it, it was like rocking a rocking chair.

We became so expert that we could fell a tree wherever we wanted, on a marker if one was set up, or in such a way that it would be nicely propped up for trimming and cutting into four foot lengths. *Timber*, the shout echoes in the clearing; *timber*, and a lord of the forest begins to fall, slowly at first and creaking, creaking louder as it rushes with a desperate clawing at the sky towards the earth; *timber*, and the giant crashes amid a splitting, swirling turmoil of broken branches, and a small cloud of fragrant mist. For the woods of winter were drenched in the perfumes of Lebanon, the sweet smell of cedar, the sharper scent of pine, the cloying resin and the other odours of dank and mouldering vegetation. I remember the fragrance of the forest because the Pacific Coast has always had two dimensions for me: its sights and its scents, with the latter sometimes stronger than the former.

There was a sense of achievement in cutting the wood and splitting it and piling it in cords along the rough logging road that climbed over the moss-covered, rocky outcrop into the tall timber; the stand was further from the highway than Gilroy (or was it Murphy?) said, which in the end, limited our operation. Much of the time it rained, but we gloried in the weather; we were soaked to the skin, the water running down our faces and necks into our clothes, but we were never sick. Good old Mother Nature, I never felt so pagan close to her. This was the life all right, working in the woods — and only the truck was vile.

Sunny Gilroy (he had been given the papal name of Urban, which he eschewed although he wasn't such a bad RC) said that he could get us a truck and kept his word; it was a rickety A model Ford, which wasn't so old but had been badly used; its springs were shot, so that we could carry only a cord at a time. Then, the logging road was not much more than a trail. We had to pile brush on the soft spots and many a time, we had to push the truck and were struck by a shotgun blast of pebbles and mud from the spinning rear wheel. "Jesus X. Christ, you son of a bitch," we cursed the old jalopy, and the cussing made us feel better. Then the engine would stop, and while we regarded ourselves as expert woodsmen and regular Paul Bunyans, we were no mechanics; we would stand around in the rain, grumbling and taking turns swinging the handle, and suddenly, for no reason, it would start. On one delivery run, we backed into a brand new Essex, denting its back fender; we had no insurance so we had to pay for the repairs in kind, which meant a couple of cords of wood.

Then, my brother slashed his wrist on the crosscut saw. We had been sawing four-foot lengths when Richard leaned across to remove a twig from the teeth; something distracted him and he dragged the underpart of his forearm across the razor-sharp edges. The blood spurted out, splashing against the saw and forming a pool on the ground, and my brother, who was younger and bigger than I, went white. We quickly applied a tourniquet, using a handkerchief and a stick, and stopped the bleeding. Half a dozen stitches were needed to close the wound and the doctor took a cord of wood in payment.

It wasn't because of this second accident that we decided to pack up the lumbering venture, but because we had run out of timber that was easily accessible. In order to continue, we would have had to extend the logging road and we didn't figure it was worth it for the money we were making. As things turned out, shortly afterward I started work on the *Victoria Daily Times.*

7

In my forlorn quest for a job, I had visited both papers in Victoria — and it was largely because of the encouragement of old Ben Nicholas that to be a reporter became my overwhelming ambition, since, prior to this, I hadn't been so keen about journalism. It was true that I had written for the *McGill Daily* on occasion, but that was as a publicist more than anything else, as I was promoting the rowing club and the English rugby club in which I was also interested. Now, the glamour and adventure of the news business got me and I took to reading books about journalism. One that fascinated me was *Hot News* by Emile Gavreau; it was about a New York tabloid in the twenties where sensationalism was carried to the point of inventing news and assembling composite pictures of such deliciously improper subjects as King George having a bath — oh boy, what a crazy and exciting world it was, and I longed to be part of it.

However, I wasn't going to get far with the editor of the *Daily Colonist*; that was apparent from my first and only interview. "Pinkie" McKelvie was a heavyset man with black hair that was turning gray and a grizzled moustache, and the pink cheeks which provided his nickname; he looked dyspeptic and somewhat surly the night that I saw him — and I saw him at night for the *Colonist* was a morning paper. His office in the ugly red brick monstrosity on View Street that housed the *Colonist* had been painted a mint green colour; not a picture hung on the wall, and the room had an antiseptic air.

There was no opening on the *Colonist,* Pinkie said firmly and finally, and there wouldn't be for years and years, in his opinion, as the whole newspaper business was foundering and going down the drain. In any case, he went on, one had to have experience to be a reporter, and he wasn't running a kindergarten in this shop, and that was that and good-night.

What a contrast between this and the way the editor of the *Victoria Daily Times* received me! It was not so much what he said, but his warm and genial presence. Mr. Nicholas was a round rubber ball of a man with a great moon face, the colour of old ivory, which shone with kindness and understanding, or so it seemed to me. Goddammit, he was interested in me where all the others I had seen in my desperate search for a job were not and would have liked to get rid of me; he wanted to know all about me, and while I jabbered on Benny sat in his swivel chair like a benevolent Buddha. There was nothing at the moment, he said, but . . . and I was elevated on the wings of hope.

The editor's office was on the fourth floor of the Times Building, a five story block on the corner of Fort and Broad streets. You stepped off the cage elevator and to the right was a dark, shabby cloakroom, made of partitions, that divided the editorial sanctum from the news room which, from the glimpses I had of it through the open door, was a noisy, untidy place, the floor littered with papers. There was a reception room before the editor's office, and a dark youth, Irving Strickland, sat in a sort of sheep pen; he seemed a formidable figure to me then, and I had to steel myself to ask him if the editor were in and I could see him.

B. C. (Benjamin Charles) Nicholas had an old roll-top desk which was piled high with papers, the lower strata of which were yellowing with age; as he typed his editorials, there was a typewriter on his desk, or when not in use, balanced precariously on one of the lesser piles of paper. Benny liked a cigar but he chewed rather than smoked it, and beside his editorial chair was a brass spittoon of which he made regular and expert use, expectorating a pale yellow quid that plopped almost always dead centre. The only other furniture in this dingy room was a couple of wooden chairs and a table piled high with another slag heap of papers. On the gray walls were two framed photographs, usually hanging askew; one was of the founder of the *Victoria Daily Times*, a bewhiskered gentleman by name of William Templeman, who had been a temporary politician and served in the Laurier Ministry; Benny had accompanied him to Ottawa and acted as his executive assistant.

8

When at last I got a job, it wasn't the thrill that I expected to leave the dismal void of unemployment. Oh, there was a warm feeling of relief all right, but no overwhelming desire to kick up one's heels and shout whoopee. The reason was that my transition was so slow: it took literally months for me to become a full time reporter on the *Victoria Daily Times*, and this was because I had started on a part-time, two-to-three-days-a-week, basis.

It was on a dark afternoon in the early spring of 1934 that Benny Nicholas got around to offering me work as an "outside" reporter, writing mainly for a new farm and garden page that was going to be part of the weekly feature section. By "outside", the editor meant that I would do most of my work outside the office, only coming in a couple of days at the end of the week to edit the page and see it in print. I remember the light was on in his office, and it shone on the bald pate of his humpty-dumpty figure, perched on the edge of his swivel chair. The pay would be thirty dollars a month, and Benny said that he would have liked to do better. From that, I gathered that the Liberal Party hadn't been as generous as he had expected, because the editor had earlier taken me into his confidence, perhaps to keep my spirits up, and told me that the paper might be getting some money from the party, and he might be able to carry out some of his plans for expansion. (The Liberals had recently come to power in British Columbia, and in those days, a party paper like the *Victoria Times* could expect to benefit.)

Mr. Nicholas had to make some arrangements before I could begin and told me to see him again in a week's time, but when I asked for him seven days later, Irving Strickland said that he was away sick. Poor Irving, if he knew how much I distrusted him, but he was telling the truth, the editor was away from his office for several days. It wasn't till three weeks later that I started work. My regular stint was two articles a week for the farm and garden page; one was signed with my initials, the other had the by-line "Ceres", which was Benny's choice and he was to chortle about this, as Ceres was a goddess: it was like getting a bull mixed up with a cow, which I once did in a caption.

So, I had a job, but it was so much of an anticlimax, and it didn't happen the way I had dreamed it would. In September, 1934 I was taken on staff as a regular reporter, although I continued to do the farm and garden page; I was paid fifteen dollars a week.

9

At half past seven of a morning, the dilapidated news room of the *Victoria Daily Times* appeared to be clean and even smelled fresh from the disinfectant that Joe had used in his janitoring the night before. The sports editor had been at work for a half-hour or more, as the sports page had an early deadline, and almost always, Archie Wills was at his desk, marking and clipping the morning newspaper, before the first reporter stepped off the creaking elevator cage after it had come to a whining stop.

In his capacity as a combined news editor and city editor, Archie was Benny's right-hand man and had worked on the paper all his life. For some reason, perhaps because of the overwhelming integrity which was a result of his upbringing, he took the opposite course to the roistering crowd on the newspapers in those days: he didn't smoke or drink. Archie Wills would hand out the clippings for rewrites (they were obituaries or meetings which weren't worth covering), and make out the day's assignments, scrawling them in an old-fashioned ledger on his desk, which Lionel and I would check after we had done our stint on the telegraph desk.

That was the first job, scanning the world news that had come clattering into the Canadian Press cubbyhole next door; Bill Henderson would tear the copy into the right lengths with a steel ruler and hand us reports to edit and head up. The telegraph editor was a deceptively mild looking man, with his pince nez glasses perched on an upturned nose, thinning gray hair and a clipped moustache, for we knew him as a blasphemous iconoclast and revolutionary. Now and then, when he was in his cups, he would break out of his Milquetoast mould and become a raging lion, to the stunned amazement of his friends. "He has a big mind," Lionel would say, although he hinted darkly that he might be a Trotzkyist which, I gathered, was the worst kind of heretic.

Bill Henderson belonged to the old breed of newspapermen who led a nomadic life, moving from town to town, seldom spending more than a year on any one paper, and then off again to the next place, which was so much like the last place. There was a tradition among editors that these journalistic hoboes should be given a couple of weeks work even if there were none, but that died with the depression, and Bill had the good sense to settle in Victoria. If he were in the mood after the last deadline had passed, he would talk about the papers he had worked for: they were not all in Canada, for this traffic knew no boundaries except that of language. There were papers in the South, he said, that were "so goddam lily-white that the shithouses didn't have to be segregated", and he had worked in Chicago in the rip-roaring twenties when police reporters carried guns and some were even members of the mobs. Bill Henderson learned his politics the hard way, by knocking around the continent, and he had nothing but contempt for liberals and reformers whom he lumped together as a "Jeezeling bunch of smarmy do-gooders".

By eight o'clock, the editor had stepped out of the rickety elevator and unlocked the outer door of his office. His great oval face was freshly shaved and he exuded an aroma which was a subtle blend of eau de cologne, lavender-scented soap and Havana cigars; he seemed renewed and refreshed of a morning, and he always enjoyed his walk to work on a fine day from his apartment near Craigdarroch, the coal miner's castle on a commanding hill in the middle of Victoria, whose turrets and banquetting halls were occupied by Victoria College.*

Benjamin Charles Nicholas was born in the mining camp of Virginia City, Nevada, the son of a Cornish miner, but the accident of birth didn't make him an American for long. As a child, he was taken to Seattle and then to Victoria. He had a better-than-average education, considering the times and the fact that there was no university in British Columbia when he grew up; he followed the usual course: he delivered papers and worked summers as a store clerk and then, because he felt that he had a flair for writing, started as a copy boy and cub reporter on the *Victoria Daily Times*.

His opportunity came when he was made marine reporter — much of the news of the Orient was gleaned from the latest Hong Kong, Shanghai and Tokyo English language papers aboard the Canadian Pacific "White Empresses" and the Japanese NYK liners which made Victoria their first port of call in crossing the Pacific. There was no wireless and the telegraph was too expensive for any detailed reporting; in any case, as Benny said, what happened to the Chinks and Wogs wasn't considered worth a cable toll. So, the reporters went out on the pilot boat, the whole rapscallion crowd, and boarded the liner off William Head and worked and drank, for the pursers were always lavish with the duty free liquor, until they came staggering off at Rithet's pier with half a dozen stories apiece.

*Predecessor of the University of Victoria.

30

On the ship, the reporter's first request was for the files, the newspaper files. When Archie Wills got the marine beat, he looked such a kid, and he wasn't more than nineteen, that all sorts of tricks were played on him. The first time he asked for the files — and he had been told to do this when he was given the assignment — the captain transmitted the order to the mate with a wink. In a couple of minutes, the officer was back with a bunch of large, rusty iron files. The captain slapped his sides and offered the boy a drink but he wouldn't have one; in fact, he wouldn't even have a ginger ale on one of these mail boats, in case it was spiked.

Even now it was a good beat, the editor said while talking shop one day in his office. Although the files didn't count for as much, there were always the interviews with the captain and the personalities among the passengers. There were interviews in the old days too, and a broad grin lit up Benny's moon face as he recalled an escapade of John Shaw's, which might have been apocryphal as John Shaw was a news room legend, although he was real enough and worked in Hong Kong on one of the papers there. At any rate, he was on the *Times* marine beat when a certain Chinese general, known as Laughing Wu to distinguish him from another Wu, was expected aboard the *Empress of Russia* — or was it the *Empress of Asia*? The local Chinese benevolent association, which was going to act as his host, had been informed of his movements and let the paper know.

If there was a chance of getting the stories into the paper that day, the *Times* would send an office boy to Rithet's pier to run the copy back, and "we did so that time," Ben Nicholas said, as the *Empress* docked before noon. The office boy stood at the end of the gangplank and watched one reporter after another come staggering down, but no John Shaw: he became alarmed as the time ticked toward the deadline of the first edition. Finally, John Shaw appeared and lurched down the gangplank.

"Nothing today, boy," he said thickly, and the editor put on a drunken accent; "nothing that won't stand up till tomorrow and can't be written later in the office."

"But, what about the interview with Laughing Wu," the office boy wailed. "The city editor is waiting for that story and told me to be sure to get it."

"Oh that," said John Shaw, and putting a hand in his inside pocket, he pulled out a wad of dirty copy paper which he handed over, muttering that he had forgotten about it because he had written it before going aboard the *Empress*. With that, the great reporter left a rather puzzled office boy and made his unsteady way across the dock.

It was true, Benny said, that there was a sameness about the shipboard interview with celebrities. Any good reporter could write one from memory — there would be the usual platitudes: the big shot was delighted to be visiting Victoria which he had heard was a Little Bit of Old England, he was impressed with the beauty of Vancouver Island or what he had seen, and remarked about the great prospects facing British Columbia, and so on. There was nothing wrong with John Shaw's interview except that it could never have occurred. Laughing Wu was not on the ship; he had stopped over in Japan. But what was really bad luck was that he had got into such a row with the Japanese that it had hit the headlines on the day after the "interview" with him had been played up on the front page of the *Victoria Daily Times*.

Mr. Nicholas never said what happened to John Shaw; a paroxysm of mirth rippled down his clothes and interrupted his narrative. Was the reporter fired or was he one of the members of the staff who had been fired and immediately rehired? All that the editor would say was that John Shaw was doing very well.

Benny had been a marine reporter at the time of the Russo-Japanese War, which was as good as being a foreign correspondent at Port Arthur or Darien or Tokyo. Newspapers in Vancouver and Seattle and as far away as Portland, and even the *New York Times*, it was said, sent reporters to Victoria whenever a great ship from the Orient was expected. As a result of his secondhand coverage of that war from the liners' three-week-old newspaper files, the young Ben Nicholas received offers from several big papers in Canada and the United States.

He was tempted by this chance of fame and fortune, and who wouldn't be, but at the same time, he was frightened; he was afraid of the unknown, but most of all he was afraid that his mother would not want to move and while he found her apron strings restrictive and even complained about them on occasion, there was all the cosy comfort of the home she provided and he could not imagine living without her. Mrs. Nicholas never stood in the way of her son's advancement; in fact, she encouraged him to take the new job, although she did speak of the hustle and bustle of the big city and its anonymity. It wasn't difficult for Benny to make up his mind: he chose familiarity, the folks next door and friends on the street, intriguing back yard gossip, the petty causes of an outpost, its silly quarrels and ridiculous reconciliations, and he never regretted it.

Everyone knew the editor of the *Times*, and he revelled in his local fame; he would wave to this person and shout a greeting at that person and stop to chat with another as he slowly walked to the office, for Benny loved people as only a lonely bachelor does. He always carried a package of boiled sweets for the little boys whom he met and who knew him and would shout out "Hiya Benny", which pleased him enormously. His eyes would be twinkling by the time he reached the Times Building and his flat-footed waddle had a bounce.

Between eight and ten of a morning, the editor was engaged in writing editorials, and this was the only time when the door to his office was shut, and Irving Strickland refused to allow anyone to enter. Then Benny chewed on his cigar, rattled a peppermint around his mouth, grunted, muttered to himself, fed copy paper into his ancient typewriter, tore it out, put in more, typed, and finally produced a comment which satisfied him and which he got Irving to send up the chute from the news room to the linotype room upstairs.

At 10 A.M., there was the daily conference which Archie Wills attended, as well as W. A., Bill, Patterson, the advertising manager, a quiet-spoken man with premature white hair, and V. B., Billie, Monteith, the accountant and business manager, an extraordinary Victorian figure, lanky, skeletal, with a great display of yellow teeth like antique piano keys, and thick glasses. They sat on the hard wooden chairs in front of the beat-up, old roll-top desk, and they enjoyed themselves because Benny spent most of the time yarning about the British remittance men and their antics, and the latest adventure of the Australian con man. It was a continuous serial told by a master story teller, and why worry about the day-to-day business of bringing out a newspaper.

10

Some time after I started work on the *Victoria Daily Times*, Pinkie McKelvie, the editor of the *Colonist* who had so brusquely turned me down, joined the ranks of the unemployed. It was a startling development and, we heard, all due to his insistence on campaigning for a lost cause. For, beneath the tough "Front Page" exterior, Bruce A. "Pinkie" McKelvie was an ardent and extraordinarily sentimental local historian who was convinced that Vancouver Island had been much better off when it was a colony — that was its golden age. Since then, it had been exploited by the covetous mainland of British Columbia, squeezed to pulp, sucked dry. Oh yes, Victoria had been made the capital of the province, but it had gone down, it had declined in stature. Vancouver was the big city, four or five times as large — Vancouver, the contemptible Gastown, which had been no more than a clearing in the forest when Victoria had outfitted the Cariboo and Yukon Gold Rushes and had ruled, as the Great Queen had ruled, in majesty over the vast Pacific Northwest.

If Vancouver Island were independent, Victoria would flourish again as a free port, Pinkie said, and he proposed that Vancouver Island should revert to the status of a crown colony, that it had before it joined the mainland to form the province of British Columbia. As editor, he made use of the pages of the *Colonist* (aptly named) to advocate secession, which might have been dismissed as a delightful eccentricity if it hadn't been for the depression, and the search for any kind of solution. Maybe this was the way to bring back prosperity to Victoria which, God knows, was badly off.

At any rate, Pinkie became more and more rabid on the subject; he and his cronies held meetings, and there was excited gossip that he was forming a political party and that he would be marching down Government Street at the head of it, with banners calling for the separation of the island from the mainland. (Later he did form the Vancouver Island Provincial Association which, however, never contested an election.) Pinkie saw an independent Vancouver Island becoming the Monte Carlo

of the Western Hemisphere, and said so in the pages of the *Colonist* —
and the paper's name took on a new meaning for its readers. He even
suggested that the provincial parliament buildings in Victoria might be
turned into a casino!

Meanwhile, the Matsons, who were the publishers and owners of the
Colonist, were becoming more and more restive; they didn't find it funny
when their wealthy mainland friends charged them, even while kidding,
with subversion. Finally they ordered the editor to "cease and desist",
but the separatist movement had gone so far that there was nothing for
Pinkie to do but quit. At least, that was the local scuttlebutt. Nothing
official was said, proprietors could be close-mouthed in those days, and
all that appeared in the *Colonist* of May 2, 1937 was that he was leaving
and fellow members of the editorial department had made him a presen-
tation. Besides Pinkie McKelvie, there were other saviours who wanted
to lead the people out of the depths of the depression to prosperity.
Of course, Pinkie, with his vision of an independent Vancouver Island,
the Monte Carlo of the Pacific Coast, was a local phenomenon, but
there were self-anointed messiahs with a much broader appeal, and all
of them had their say.

Major C. H. Douglas, the founder of Social Credit, was one: he was
the perfect example of a prophet not being without honour save in his
own country. In Alberta they worshipped him, and his chief apostle,
Bible Bill Aberhart, was so successful in spreading the Social Credit
doctrine that he was elected to put it into force and called on his mentor
to show how it should be done; Douglas also had disciples in New
Zealand; but in the old country, they wouldn't give him the time of day.
Major Douglas picked up a number of converts on Vancouver Island
among the tweedy British fruit farmers, who were first attracted to his
funny money theories by the fact that he was an officer and presumably
a gentleman. Actually, the major was embarrassed by his fundamentalist
followers in Alberta and engaged in doctrinal disputes with Bible Bill
and his disciples.

Then, there was the slender, white-haired, Dr. Francis E. Townsend
with his Old Age Revolving Pension Plan, the Townsend Plan, which
had some of the features of Social Credit in its financing. The Townsend
Plan was an American plan but it had a tremendous appeal for the old
people of whom Victoria had more than its share — after all, Victoria
was the place where people came to die, it was the only graveyard with
lights, ha ha! We heard over the radio about Upton Sinclair and his
plan to "End Poverty In California", the EPIC plan which he outlined
in a pamphlet that must have sold more copies than all his novels com-

bined — and good God, he almost made it as *I, governor of California, and how I ended poverty.**

However, the messiah, or anti-messiah, who went over best on Vancouver Island and throughout British Columbia, was Howard Scott, the head of Technocracy Inc. Long after the war replaced the depression, and even after the war ended, there were men wearing gray shirts and gray suits and driving cars painted silver gray along the lanes of the island, and there was an abandoned church in downtown Vancouver which had served as a local headquarters for the movement and bore the legend "Technocracy Inc." above its doric wooden columns until quite recently.

I heard Howard Scott speak in Victoria's City Temple, which looked more like a large hall than a church, and whose pastor encouraged public meetings on the issues of the times: Rev. Clem Davies, a pint-sized Welsh evangelist, was one clergyman who was not afraid of discussing the depression and politics, although he didn't have a very clear idea of what was happening — but then, who did? He was a popularizer more than anything else, and it was a measure of his successful ministry that the City Temple was always full. I remember one jam-packed meeting when the Reverend Mr. Davies talked portentously about Hitler and the National Socialists and how people everywhere were becoming socialists because of the "international bankers" (the main scapegoat of the thirties) and the way they were prolonging the depression. His confusion was shared by his audience, and it wasn't till later that I learned that the Nazis were not socialists. Clem Davies became Victoria's first radio priest and began to sound like Father Coughlin after a time.

Howard Scott was a big handsome man who wore a light gray suit, a silver gray tie, and had prematurely gray hair. He had an overwhelming confidence that the world belonged to scientists and engineers like himself, the technologists as he called them, and was contemptuous of the rest of mankind, "the morons", he said — why, at the last election, "forty million morons had made the United States safe for Tammany". (He must have visited Victoria after the 1932 election but before Roosevelt was sworn in.) He proclaimed that progress was in a direct ratio to the approach of the outer wall of the stomach to the backbone, and he had other aphorisms, such as: "There is just as much chance of America paying its debts as of a celluloid dog catching an asbestos cat in Hades"; his definition of a criminal was a "man with predatory instincts but insufficient capital to start a corporation".

So far, this was rabble rousing on a high intellectual plane, but then

*The actual title of Sinclair's election pamphlet, subtitled "a true story of the future", 1933, New York, Farrar, Strauss.

Howard Scott talked about the new currency which was to be based on energy rather than on "useless gold". I was fascinated, although I had to admit that I didn't understand all this stuff about ergs and joules (dim recollections of Physics II at McGill), which were to replace dollars and cents. Apparently, these ergs and joules were so much advanced on the old greenbacks and spondulics that they could be personalized and would be different for males and females, and couldn't be lent or given away but had to be spent. Wow, what an idea, but it was baffling. Everyone would get the same income, Howard Scott said, because it would "cost too much" to have a graduated scale of salaries. It was absolutely super-duper marvellous.

There was something about Howard Scott that reminded me of Lionel Backler; perhaps, it was his confidence, even arrogance, his air of certainty that he had all the answers — only Lionel claimed he didn't and called him a charlatan. All of which might be true, I said, but people like Howard Scott and Dr. Townsend had done a service in that they had awakened the public to the fact that the United States was potentially the richest country in the world, and yet eighty percent of its people were forced to live just above the starvation level, in needless poverty. I was quoting Bruce Bliven.* But Lionel said Howard Scott was nothing but an authoritarian son of a bitch, that what he wanted was a corporate state like Mussolini's, and that engineers, who were idiots in any case, were the greatest supporters of totalitarianism alive.

We were standing ankle deep in waste paper, chewing the rag after the last edition had gone; there was no one else in the littered news room but Archie Wills, who was typing his diary and paid no attention to us. The slanting rays of light from the late afternoon sun made the shabby wooden desks with their beat-up old typewriters look like golden galleons floating on a stormy sea. "Cor Lumme, Look at the mess," said Joe the janitor, a north country Englishman, but he said that every time he came into the news room to sweep up. Striped awnings shaded the windows, which looked over the roof tops and chimney pots down Fort Street to the inner harbour, where there was an enticing glimpse of the ships with their white superstructures and brightly painted funnels; they were only ferry boats but even they had the promise of romance and adventure.

*Editor of *The New Republic* and leading liberal thinker.

11

It was at a tea party in an apartment on Beach Drive that I met Aileen, my dream girl, or said "hello" to her, as that was all that happened. Tea and buttered toast and small cakes and cucumber sandwiches, moist and yummy, and the shining sea across the road dappling the ceiling and part of one wall with globular patterns — glob, glob, you almost felt you were in an aquarium. A tea party was a tea party in the thirties and not an excuse to drink, for the pall of the depression still hung over the frightened middle classes, and liquor was a luxury that was not squandered in the daytime. Then, a tea party was the right thing to do because it was the British thing to do.

And the British: the remittance men, the old China hands like my father and Mr. Lee, the burra sahibs of the Indian Civil Service and their mem sahibs, the retired Malayan or African policemen, the former tea planters from Ceylon and the rubber planters from Borneo, the Empire builders and the Empire holders, the ex-merchants of Hong Kong and Shanghai and Bombay — it was their trade that the flag followed, on the road to Mandalay, where the old flotilla lay — and the gunboat crews and the veterans of the imperial forces in the Far East and the Near East and the East-is-East; also the battier British, those who regarded themselves as the chosen race and had some measurements in a pyramid to prove it, the British Israelites, and the more recent Oxford Groupers (who became the Moral Rearmament Association); the British were the élite in Victoria, B.C., there was no doubt about that.

The dominance of these Empire-minded British, and the fact that so many had come straight from the old country or from imperial posts, produced the British Columbia English accent, which was more or less accepted as the regional accent before the Second World War. This accent had its affect on such immigrants as the people from the prairies, who, because of the depression, were retiring to British Columbia rather than to California: it helped to soften their twang, although it did not change the grating, nutmeg-grinder voice of Elmore Philpott,* who was to come out from Ontario later in the thirties.

Many acquired the English accent without ever having set foot in

*Late broadcaster and newspaper columnist who was Liberal MP for Vancouver South 1953-57.

England, or for that matter, travelled farther than Seattle or Vancouver. There was my friend Tony Pinhorn, although it must be said of him that his parents were from England; still, he had been raised on Vancouver Island but spoke with as ripe a British public school boy accent as any "chirper" straight off the boat. So British was British Columbia in those days that English Rugby was played in all the schools, and American football was unknown and looked down on as an eastern depravity in which the players had to wear pads and crash helmets because they were afraid of getting hurt. In many ways, Victorians were more British than Canadian, and Tony Pinhorn was to join the Royal Air Force and die in the Second World War fighting for Britain. (Of course, things were changing, and the *Times* news room was a place where idols were broken, but radicals like Lionel Backler were more internationalist than nationalist.)

No wonder, then, that Victorians in the thirties should drink tea, even the newly arrived Victorians with the dust of the prairies still on their boots. The social pages of the newspapers listed those who "poured" at the parties in the great wooden mansions of Rockland or the long, low modern homes in the Uplands, and, if they were phoned, in the box-like bungalows of Saanich. Tea drinking reached the stage of a great social ritual at the Empress Hotel, where tea was served every afternoon at four o'clock in the main dining room and the vast carpeted lobby outside with its palm trees and its flowers and Billy Tickle and his string quartet in one corner. When Billy Tickle played "Land of Hope and Glory", you knew that this was the real heart of the British Empire and that the sun *couldn't* set.

I forget who had that tea party on Beach Avenue but we were delicately drinking from Royal Doulton china, and talking about the Hauptmann Trial* — the hostess, whoever she was, wanted to know the latest "disgusting" detail, — when the doorbell rang. One of the guests opened the door, and there was Aileen in a white sweater over a white pleated skirt, bobby socks and sneakers; she was on her way to play tennis and had come to borrow a racket. With a "hello" and a "goodbye" she was gone, but I had met her; the bell-shaped tones of her voice attested to her being an actress and I knew that she was one of the leading ladies in local amateur dramatics. However, it was the freshness of her appearance that remained with me, her shining cheeks, her sparkling blue eyes: radiance was the word for Aileen — she was the embodiment of youth and springtime.

*Bruno Richard Hauptmann, an immigrant carpenter, was found guilty of the kidnapping and murder of the infant son of Charles A. Lindbergh after a sensational trial. Although he protested his innocence to the end, he went to the electric chair.

1935

12

A full moon shone on the night of the fancy dress party, outlining Cadboro Bay and shimmering on the oily blackness of the sea: clouds scudded past — it was only a paper moon, dum-te-dum — and the Yacht Club looked goddam unreal, like some Hollywood mansion, with its windows all lit up and the lawns around it glistening and spooky, and the mysterious darkness beyond, where you sensed the water but all you saw was the red and green twinkle of the boats at the dock. There was a sound of excitement, the babble of voices, the insistent rhythm of the band beating out the marvellous tunes of the thirties. It was only a paper moon, shining over a cardboard sea — but boy oh boy, this wasn't make-believe.

We were out for a good time that night, and we sniffed the rich bitch smell of the Uplands that was a subtle blend of the well-kept wallflowers and roses and the usual deep-down sea stench; it was a heady perfume. Most of the shining new houses in the Uplands belonged to bootleggers — or so Ben Nicholas said, although he might have been kidding, but some of them did. There were several millionaires in Victoria who had made their pile out of rum running. I parked the old rattletrap of a Chevy roadster I had outside the Yacht Club. There were the latest 1935 models to the right and left of me, but to hell with them: if I knew the social set-up, they had been borrowed from parents, who had lent them with the greatest reluctance, whereas this was my car, my first car. I had paid thirty-five dollars for the jalopy (it was my first real purchase after getting a job). Even if it were held together with haywire and chewing gum, it went, and what was more important provided a love nest on wheels, although the hood leaked and water dripped down one's neck at moments of passion.

Among the happy crowd of boys and girls who piled out of the Chevy roadster (the usual number was eight) was my brother, and he drew attention to the two ends of a horse which passed us on its way to the Yacht Club. As they went by, the rear end, which must have had some sort of horn attached to the tail, gave off a few ripe farts. We thought this was hilariously funny and rolled around shouting with laughter, at least the boys did; the girls tried to hide their giggles.

The Yacht Club was reverberating to the rhythm of Len Acres' augmented band, and the ten pieces were too much for the size of the trophy room, so that the fancifully dressed dancers were caught up in the pounding surf of the sound and tossed hither and yon. "The music goes 'round and around whoa-ho-ho-ho-ho-ho and it comes up here, wah, wah, wah," and the three trumpeters were on their feet blasting at the ceiling, "wah, wah, wah". There was a shuddering thrill on the dance floor.

Now the brass was down, and the walls of the Yacht Club hadn't fallen, and the orchestra slid into a lilting lament. We were dancing cheek to cheek, and my partner was half-humming, half-singing, in my ear: "Git along li'l dogie, git along, git along, I'm aheading for the last round-up". What the hell was a dogie anyway? Was there one on the floor? There was a female cat, and some long-eared rabbits, also female, and a couple of wolves, male, and that horse which had broken in two with the two parts too busy wrestling with their partners, who seemed to be from a harem, to bother about that obscene horn in its tail — ha ha, Miss Fiditch my old school teacher, and nertz to Hertz and to you, you bastard, stop bumping me. There were certainly enough cowboys and cowgirls around for a round-up, including one idiot wearing a pair of silver spurs. Then I saw Aileen. She had her back to us, but I recognized her immediately, and the room was brighter, the party gayer, and everything more intense.

After a certain hour (I think it was eleven o'clock) "cut-ins" were allowed at Yacht Club dances. The stags milled around the entrance to the trophy room and I noticed that many of them were not in fancy dress and had probably crashed the party. As soon as my partner was picked off me, I was free to cut in on Aileen, which I did pronto before any of those drugstore sheikhs could get ahead of me. She had on a crinoline dress decorated with pink ribbons, one of the costumes from *Berkeley Square*, the latest Beaux Arts production, while I was meant to be a pirate and had a brightly coloured bandanna around my head, which kept coming undone.

You were supposed to have a smooth line if you were a reporter, but mine collapsed at the critical moment, and all I could think of saying was; "Where have you been all my life?" Her reply was just as inane: "Just waiting for you." But we were thrilled. "Isn't it a lovely party?" And it sure was, with the band playing "Stormy Weather", which was already a classic, and Aileen so light on her feet that we seemed to be dancing on air. This was the first time we had been together, and to me she was a dream walking.

At the Yacht Club, the only places where you could drink were in the parked cars or in the yachts and boats tied up to the dock. When the trumpeters sounded the end of that dance, we slipped away from the trophy room, through the screened porch, where couples were cuddling and smooching in dark corners, out the double doors and across the silver lawn to the old jalopy, which was half-hidden in the darkness shed by a large arbutus tree. The mickey of rye, which was the only bottle among the eight of us (most of us didn't drink and those who did had only just started), was in the glove compartment: it was still half-full. I gagged on the raw liquor but Aileen swallowed hers without choking. The drink acted as a catalyst, and after this one hasty swig, we drew closer and began to neck.

Zowie! But who would have thunk it?

13

Once upon a time, Victoria was the Hollywood of Canada, and this is no fairy story. Reporting on the film production in the Willows Fair Ground was one of my first assignments as a full time reporter for the *Times*. I am not referring to the feature-length movie the Dunsmuirs had made in the early thirties in which one of the Dunsmuir girls had a leading role: it was called *The Purple Passion* or *The Crimson Paradise* or something like that, and had its world première in Victoria, which was a glittering social success, according to the newspaper accounts — there was some question as to whether this film was ever shown again. No, this was in the winter of 1934–35, when an American company tried to take advantage of changes in the British quota law and made a couple of films on Vancouver Island (they would be accepted under the quota as British made).

These pictures featured players like David Manners, Maxine Doyle, Lyle Talbot, Wendy Barrie, and the young Rita Hayworth, who may not have been stars of the first magnitude but were nevertheless stars. I remember David Manners had the lead in a Hollywood film called *The Crooner.**

It was a glamorous assignment and helped me out with Aileen, who was a representative girl and as such, wanted to get into pictures like all the rest of the dumb dolls. Mind you, she had quite the wrong idea about me, which was the fault of the Hollywood characters and the way they treated the press, even a cub reporter like me. I mean David Manners and Maxine Doyle always seemed to be pleased to see me, and the director, whose name I've forgotten, would put his hand on my shoulder as he squinted through the focusing lens of the camera, and it looked as though he were consulting me. As a result, Aileen thought I had a lot of influence and begged me to get her a part. I did speak to the director, who gave her a bit part where she spoke a line — you know, something memorable like: "Isn't it a wonderful day?" That pleased her, but when the film was shown some months later (I think it was in April or May of 1935) at another world première in Victoria,

---

*Manners was Canadian born and educated. His Victoria-made film with Maxine Doyle was *Lucky Fugitive*.

I didn't see Aileen and I figured that she had finished up on the cutting room floor, and I wondered whether the director hadn't intended that to happen all the time.

For the few lucky ones like Aileen who spoke a few words, the pay was five dollars a day, and the day began at six o'clock in the morning and lasted till late at night. It took them all one morning to shoot her miserable sequence, and she was on call for several days afterwards. The regular extras were paid two dollars a day, while the crowd extras got only one dollar a day, for which they had to turn out in light summer frocks and clothes for an outdoor garden party scene which was being shot on a chilly winter's day; they drank ice water to keep their breath from steaming. The wages were low even for the thirties, and there was no doubt that the director, who was a likeable rogue, was playing the Beaux Arts members for suckers, but the fact is that most of them would gladly have worked for nothing.

Actually, it was the weather more than anything else that turned the American film makers away from making Victoria the regular Canadian Hollywood, where they might have made all their quota pictures; apparently, they expected to be able to shoot outdoors in warm sunny weather during the winter on Vancouver Island, just as they could do in southern California.

The Willows Fair Ground was the film lot, as they called it, although there was a certain amount of shooting on location: on one of the ferries tied up for the winter, out at Ten Mile Point, and elsewhere. The cattle barn, which was a rambling wreck of a wooden building with a sway-back roof, had been converted into a sound stage. There were usually four sets: a café scene with a bar and a cluster of tables and chairs which was in one corner, the big dance hall set which covered the whole end of the barn, a part of a store showing a sales counter, and an automobile without wheels, mounted on blocks. The sawn-off car, which was standard equipment with any movie company, was used for the driving sequences; a couple of stage hands waved cedar branches before the two actors in the front seat, casting flickering shadows on their faces and giving the illusion of motion while two other men rocked the wheel-less vehicle on its blocks.

I found the dancing scenes even more fascinating. The orchestra, which was probably Billy Tickle's, was out of view while the general shots were taken, but when there was any dialogue, when David Manners talked to Maxine Doyle as they danced or while dancing was going on, the music stopped, but the extras went on dancing. There were self-conscious giggles from the stage-struck kids who were the extras, but after the first bellow of "Cut" from the director's assistant and his harsh admonitions through a megaphone, they learned to mime the dancing in silence. Of course, later, the music was dubbed in as background sound.

With the klieg lights on, the whole make-believe world of the sets and sound stage was bathed in brilliance, but movie making was a dreary business: there were so many retakes, that after the eighth or ninth or tenth, the actors seemed to be going through their motions like sleepwalkers. God, how I ached with boredom as I squatted on a pile of flats or leaned against a wall watching take after take after take in that lousy, stinking, old barn. Even Aileen's miserable sequence was shot over and over again; it was not that she did not know her one line, but that she would step away from the chalk mark or the sound man wasn't satisfied with the sound or the boom mike was casting a shadow which was invisible to everyone but the cameramen, who had a hell of a time exorcising it.

There was a rigorous pursuit of perfection; it was an obsession with the technicians and gave meaning to their work on a B film. It was the reason why Hollywood movies looked so good on the screen even though there was nothing to them.

14

On the morning after the Dominion Day riot in Regina, the telegraph editor was unusually agitated as he sliced up the teletype copy with his steel ruler and sorted it out on the old wooden desk that served as a telegraph desk — behind him was a hatch to the CP office. As we pulled up our chairs, Bill Henderson kept muttering something to the effect that they'd done it. We didn't know what had happened (there was no radio news then, or we didn't listen to it), and Bill explained that "Bennett's Cossacks" had done it, that there had been a bloody riot in Regina, one man killed and hundreds injured, and scores arrested, including all the strike leaders.

"Whew," we whistled, and the clatter of the teletype machines in the CP cubbyhole took on a new urgency.

Ever since the relief camp strikers reached Regina, trouble had been expected, especially when Prime Minister Bennett rushed hundreds of Mounties there with orders to stop the "march on Ottawa". This was the greatest unemployed demonstration of the depression. Lionel Backler hailed it as a revolutionary movement, the only genuine revolutionary movement the country had known — and the quaking legislators in the capital would have agreed with him. But not Benny Nicholas. The editor liked to come into the littered news room after the last edition had gone to press for a "gabfest" when he usually tangled with Lionel who, this time, was arguing that the only way a revolution could occur in Canada was by means of a "mass march" like the unemployed march on Ottawa. Benny compared the relief camp strikers with the Bonus Army* — that had been a mass march like this one, the American veterans had ridden the freight trains, only there were many more of them, twenty thousand, ten times as many as the Canadian unemployed, and what had they achieved? Nothing. The Senate had turned them down, Mr. Nicholas said, and when the government wanted to get rid of them, General Douglas MacArthur ordered his regular troops to drive them from Washington, which they did with a few whiffs of tear gas.

*Unemployed U.S. veterans who descended on Washington in May of 1932, seeking immediate payment of bonus certificates issued for service in the First World War. They camped in Washington and remained there after the Bonus bill was defeated in Congress in mid-June. On July 28 troops were ordered to evict them.

The Regina riot had its beginning in Ottawa's decision to put the relief camps under the army. Almost immediately there was trouble, and agitators moved among the men telling them that this was the first step to conscription "to fight the bosses' war against the Soviets". In the spring, the men left the camps throughout B.C. and assembled in Vancouver; they staged sit-downs in the post office and other federal buildings and supported themselves by tin-canning.

Arthur Evans was their leader, an ordinary name for an ordinary working man, but there were hints that this was not his real name — B.C. COMMUNIST LEADER DIRECTS STRIKE said the advertisement in the *Victoria Daily Times* and other papers, paid for by the Citizens' League of British Columbia, the vigilante wing of the Vancouver Chamber of Commerce, and there was a large, dark picture of Arthur Evans in a cloth cap with the caption, "Wrecker of industry, exploiter of labour". He was responsible, according to this advertisement, for calling out "2,000 men from the Dominion Government's relief camps in British Columbia" — he and his deputy, who came from somewhere in Europe near Russia.

The relief camp strikers voted to take their case to Ottawa, and at the beginning of June, they set off on an eastbound CPR freight: the roof of every box car was "black with men", according to the teletype copy. The first stop was Revelstoke and the Canadian Press report said the strikers descended in the railway yard and "with military precision . . . formed fours and marched to Riverside Park", where they bivouacked. The news spread: an army of unemployed was moving over the Rockies onto the prairies, and the towns en route trembled at its approach and tried to buy the strikers off with a donation of one hundred dollars not to stop here, then two hundred, all right five hundred dollars.

Across the parched prairies now, two thousand men on a hundred freight cars, clickety clack, burned black by the sun, almost as black as that picture of Arthur Evans in the Citizens' League ad, clickety clack, across the drought-stricken land where nothing, not even grass, grew, clickety clack, singing their Wobbly songs. On June 14 they reached Regina, which was an RCMP town (it had been headquarters of the force), and was now heavily reinforced with Mounties who had orders to stop the march. There followed the "siege", when the strikers were prevented from boarding any trains and, inevitably, the rally and the riot. It was a cop who was killed, a Regina city detective who was working with the RCMP.

Bill Henderson always handled the main story, and he went to work that day, whispering to himself, waving his pencil and shaking it as if he were trying to shake the right words out of it. He didn't have to worry about the make-up as it was pretty well standard with a 72 point eight column headline no matter what happened, the main story running down the righthand side of the front page under a two or three column drop, with a three column cut in the shoulder and the rest of the news under two column and one column heads — there was a comfortable sameness about the appearance of the *Times* in the thirties. He threw me a dispatch from Geneva which spoke of the effort being made to restrain the Italians and prevent them from attacking Ethiopia, and almost before I had written a two column head for this story, he had grabbed it and sent it up the chute to the composing room. I had never seen the telegraph editor so flustered: he was cursing and calling on "Anaemic Jesus" as his witness that the editor had taken some of the copy, and how the hell could he be expected to get it set for the front page. Mr. Nicholas wanted to see the telegram that the Saskatchewan premier, Jimmy Gardiner,* had sent to Ottawa, protesting the police action and the attempt to force the strikers into the Lumsden Camp near Regina:

POLICE INTENTION TO FORCE UNEMPLOYED MARCHERS INTO LUMS-DEN CAMP OR STARVE THEM INTO SUBMISSION STOP THIS WILL END WITH WORSE RIOT THAN LAST NIGHT STOP THESE MEN SHOULD BE FED WHERE THEY ARE AND IMMEDIATELY DISBANDED AND SENT BACK TO CAMPS AND HOMES AS THEY REQUEST WITHOUT ANY ATTEMPT TO FORCE THEM INTO LUMSDEN AND THIS SHOULD BE DONE IN NEXT TWO HOURS STOP

As the editor admitted later, he was shocked by the wording of the telegram; it was almost insurrectionary, but there was no doubt that Jimmy Gardiner was right and that R. B. Bennett was arrogant, over-bearing, a typical high-handed Tory, but still he was prime minister of Canada. It was almost an automatic gesture for Benny to put a large unlighted cigar in his mouth when he started an editorial: the lead or first paragraph was always the hardest to write, like the lead of a news story, and after that you could rattle along, but, the editor said, there was a difference between the two in that the end of an editorial was as important as its beginning, and you had to figure out what you were going to say before you started typing — and Mr. Nicholas emphasized that an editorial should say something and not be a crappy review. By the time the editor got to the guts of an editorial, he was chewing his cigar or rolling a peppermint around in his mouth; he did a lot of x-ing on this one and even tore out one sheet and retyped it:

Premier Gardiner's recital of the proposals made by the strikers in the morning puts the immediate responsibility for the outbreak

*Later Rt. Hon. J. G. Gardiner, Minister of Agriculture.

right up to Ottawa. There was nothing in the proposals which should not have been accepted. The strikers offered to disperse and return to their camps or homes, either under their own organization or under the direction of the provincial government. The refusal of Ottawa to permit them to disperse in either of these circumstances furnishes a sinister commentary on the whole business, especially when it was followed by a charge of steel-helmeted police on an open air meeting. It is a matter which should be ventilated in Parliament at once, for it looks like deliberate provocation of trouble by the federal authorities.

It is worth noting that Premier Gardiner has protested to Ottawa against the way in which the Dominion has handled the relief camp strike situation since it shifted to Saskatchewan and which even reached the point of the federal police, under an authority of a Dominion order-in-council, going around to farmers and warning them against providing assistance to the strikers in facilitating their march eastward. After all, this is Canada, not Germany or Russia or Italy. Canada will tolerate neither fascism or communism.

There was no occasion for the frantic policy of the federal government over the relief camp strike. It is true the strikers include a number of young hotheads who no doubt have been filled with the nostrums of communism by Evans and his aides, but it is also true that they comprise a lot of good Canadians who have been made desperate by the utter hopelessness of their conditions in these camps, of waiting for jobs to "come to them" to use the classic phrase of Mr. Bennett, whose policy in creating this demoralizing atmosphere is leaving a scar on the citizenship of this country which will not be effaced for a generation . . . .

There was more in the same vein, as the editorial, which was entitled "The Clash at Regina", filled a whole column on the editorial page, and the editorial page column was wider than that on the news pages. We radicals, the "news room Reds" as we were called, were delighted that Ben Nicholas had sided with the strikers and "given the Mounties hell", and we talked about this in the Canadian Legion Club, where we went after the last edition. The club was a dirty low-ceilinged hall which stank of stale beer and piss, so much so that the first sniff almost took your breath away; it was lousy, all right, but the only place where you could get a drink (the draft ale was a nickel a glass) as there were no beer parlours in Victoria, that's what a graveyard it was. Lionel muttered darkly about the breweries and political corruption and how they were spiking the beer with chemicals.

"You should have seen the bile come up when I was sick the other night," he said.

We agreed that the Regina riot was a historic event, the beginning of the Canadian Revolution, and that the Dominion government stood revealed in all its bloodthirsty reaction, and we expressed the hope that the strikers would defy Bennett's "cossacks" and continue the march on Ottawa. They didn't, and we were disappointed at the lack of militancy shown by Arthur Evans and the leadership, but by the time the Canadian Press reported that the strikers were actually returning home to the camps in British Columbia, it was old hat, and we had really lost interest.

15

My romance with Aileen had followed the generally accepted course in Victoria: 1) the meeting at the Yacht Club fancy dress party; 2) the telephone call three or four days later (the next day would have been rushing it). Her mother answered — I was to find that she always answered — and there was her carefully cultivated voice with its hint of an English accent giving a cool welcome and singing out "Aileen". A gaily banal conversation followed and an invitation to the Saturday night dance at the Empress Hotel. That was to impress the girl; it was also an earnest of one's serious intention. Next time out: a round of the beer parlours in Esquimalt, the Canadian Navy's Pacific base, (the holier-than-thou Christians who were responsible for keeping Victoria dry could be said to have contributed to drunken driving, but I doubt if that ever preyed on their consciences). A pub crawl was a more practical tribal rite, and to put it crudely, brought the girl down to earth, literally and metaphorically speaking.

Although the Saturday night dance at the hotel was considered high society, and the *Times* devoted a column in the following Monday's social page to the names of those attending, it was not expensive even by the meagre standards of the thirties. For two dollars a couple, a three-course dinner was served with the full silver service, consommé, chicken à la King, ice cream parfait, and coffee, at tables arranged cabaret style around the magnificent ballroom with its great domed ceiling and shimmering chandeliers. When the price was raised to $2.50, as it was in 1936, there was a howl of middle class anguish and charges of profiteering.

The Canadian Pacific Railway, which owned the hotel, was not loved in British Columbia nor in the rest of the West, but it was feared. Its power was such that it frightened the local police, so that the patrons of the Saturday night dance could bring their bottles and drink at their tables — which was definitely against the blue laws of the times — in the sure knowledge that they wouldn't be pinched. Mind you, there was no vulgar flouting of the anti-drinking ordinances — the knights of the British Empire who ran the CPR wouldn't have liked that — and while the waiters provided ice and mixes as a matter of course, they insisted that the bottles when not in use should be stowed under the table. As a mickey of five-year-old rye cost $1.15 (the regular gut rot was $1 a pint), a high old night could be had for less than $5, even if we went to the Poodle Dog Café afterwards for a bowl of clam chowder, which we usually did.

The Saturday night dance at the Empress was more or less a formal affair, which helped to keep it exclusively bourgeois. You could go without a tux but you would feel out of place, although you might pass for a tourist; in summer there was a relaxation in dress, and blazers were considered quite proper, if not sports jackets, but the girls always wore long dresses.

As I warned at the beginning, Aileen was not necessarily the same girl, but although I can't say who she was (in looking back over so many years, I'm not really sure), the first time I took her to the Empress, she wore a plain white gown that fitted closely around the long curve of her hips and flared at her feet — I know that and I know too that she looked like the sun goddess with her golden tan, and that her eyes shone, and that her lips had a wet seductive look about them. There was one thing that Aileen, whoever she was, had, and that was oomph — the kind of oomph that had us always being caught in the spotlight when the lights were off and the great floor sighed to the dancing in the dark.

For this was the glorious swingtime and nature was glad we had met. Billy Tickle leaned down from the bandstand to speak to Aileen; he knew her — but for crying out loud, everyone knew her — she was the sweetheart of Sigma Chi, she was a dream walking. He knew her because they had been in concerts together, as Aileen could sing as well as act, and dance too. Billy Tickle gave her a Benny Goodman smile, and he looked like the Benny Goodman kind of jazz musician, cool, business-like, in his sharkskin dinner jacket. A transformation had come over him since the afternoon when he was Billy Tickle (or was it William Tickle?) and his string ensemble playing Viennese waltzes for the dowagers and ladies having tea and crumpets in the flower-filled lobbies and dining room of the Empress Hotel; then, he wore an old pair of tails and had a violin under his chin and looked the part of a European maestro in a British palm court. Now, with the wave of a magic baton, he was a North American big band leader, or the Victoria equivalent, and his small ensemble had grown to a ten-piece orchestra; Billy Tickle, his smile flashing, told Aileen that he was about to play her current favourite, "Cocktails for Two".

16

Of course, we talked about other things besides politics when we did the rounds of the beer parlours, but we did talk about politics, especially when it was a stag group — the girls, we found, weren't that interested in FDR and the New Deal and the growing menace of fascism in the world. We would pile into a car and head for Esquimalt and the "Coach and Horses", which tried to look like an English inn by that name. There was the "Bucket of Blood" down by the shipyards, although how it ever got that nickname I never knew, but it had a great appeal for the younger gentlewomen, who entered it all of a tremble, only to find that it was a very ordinary tavern and the side for "ladies and escorts" was decorated in the latest pub style, with chrome and plastic chairs and tables.

Beyond the city, there was the Colwood Hotel, a great echoing barn of a drinking hall. The one I liked best was on the lagoon; "The Dugout" stood amid the sand dunes and the phosphorescent flash of the surf at night. I recall a stall on the beach where a Japanese fisherman sold cooked Pacific crabs under a hissing acetylene light. Such were the ridiculous drinking laws (which we were sure had been drawn up by the brewers in an unholy alliance with the Christian temperance crowd), that you couldn't buy any food in a beer parlour, but if you could buy it outside and bring it in, then you could eat it. This was probably a loophole that the brewers had somehow overlooked — because there was no singing, no dancing, no standing, no games, no food, no entertainment in the benighted B.C. pubs, just sitting and drinking, sloshing it back glass by glass, until everyone and everything ran with beer.

As I said, radio news had made very little impact in the mid-thirties, although the Canadian Radio Broadcasting Commission had been set up, but I do recall a broadcast by Senator Huey P. Long of Louisiana, I heard it over a car radio while on a pub crawl. I don't know whose it could have been because while I had a "new" car, a 1928 Essex coupe which was a long, low, smooth job with a rumble seat, it didn't have a radio. At any rate, it was a coast-to-coast political broadcast and Senator Long was using it to the best advantage. Every five minutes, he would interrupt the flow of his rhetoric to announce in a cracker barrel voice:

"For the benefit of those who may have just tooned in, I'd like to say that this is Senator Hooey P. Long of Louisiana speaking."

It was a half-hour broadcast. Every five minutes, he would interrupt a tirade about sharing the wealth, and how every American should be a king but no one wear a crown in the great United States of America to identify himself, in his hillbilly whine: "For the benefit of those who may have just tooned in, this is . . . ." We laughed, but Lionel Backler said that Huey P. Long was beginning his campaign for the presidency with this coast-to-coast broadcast, that he was aiming at Roosevelt in '36, and that he could be dangerous. Some of us supported the Senator's proposals to close the relief camps and put everyone to work building schools, hospitals, parks and highways. Something had to be done about unemployment. We could not go on the way we were.

"Mussolini made the trains run on time," Lionel said, and added that Huey Long would do the same, that he was a one hundred percent fascist and could be the first dictator of the United States. He was the rallying point for all the reactionaries, the bigots, the Roosevelt haters, the economic royalists — and where the hell did we think he got the money for that coast-to-coast hookup? He wouldn't use gangsters or bully boys in coloured shirts to seize power, although Huey had them, he had his own private guards. The monopolists and right wingers backing him were too smart for that — he would use democracy to become a dictator. He would appear in the guise of a reformer, a man of the people, and Huey Long was that all right — he was a Democrat, and that would be the sort who would become the first American dictator. After all, Lionel Backler said, Mussolini was a socialist.

Talking about Musso, the "Eye-ties" were pretty unpopular with the Victorians because of the way they were bullying the poor, bloody Ethiopians — even the British, the retired Indian burra sahibs, the old China hands like my father, who were adept at suppressing the natives, considered it to be a "very poor show, indeed", and said so. Maybe Musso was born fifty years too late. The Italians were doing just what the British had done at the end of the nineteenth century, they had mowed down the poor, bloody Fuzzy Wuzzies, remember Kipling. Then, there was what's his name, the Emperor of the Abyssinians or the Ethiopians or whatever they called themselves — the queer looking little jerk who was some relation of the Queen of Sheba, can you beat that, Haile Selassie, that was it, the Lion of Judah, King of Kings — he wasn't out of the last century, for God's sake, he was pre-Christian, he was of the period of Nebuchadnezzar, and his warriors were armed like the Babylonians with spears. The poor buggers were going to have to fend off fascist tanks and planes.

It would be a massacre, and what the hell were we doing about it?

17

It was a long hot summer, the summer of 1935, but come to think of it, so was every summer of the thirties, which may be a result of retrospect and the warm glow thereof, but the fact is that the summers of the depression burned the forests of the Pacific Coast (there was a forest fire on Little Saanich Mountain not half a mile from our place at Royal Oak) and dried the prairies to a dustbowl.

Downtown Victoria, which wasn't much more than six city blocks, was like a brick furnace, but up around Craigdarroch, the trees stretched a leafy awning over the lanes and carriageways of the old Rockland suburb, whose gardens, with their lawns and large ornamental trees and shrubs and flower beds full of roses and antirrhinums, tall delphiniums and lilies, and sweetly scented wallflowers, were the pride of the conducted tours. They were the proof that Victoria was a "Little Bit of Olde England", as it said it was, and the bus drivers who doubled as spielers invented titles for the owners of the largest wooden mansions and the most beautiful gardens. On one tour, it would be Lord Dunsmuir who had built Craigdarroch, and on another, the Duke of Dunsmuir, and my friend George Cameron's parents were referred to as Lord and Lady Cameron (his father was a minor lumber baron, his mother reigning head of Victoria's musical life) when the bus passed their home; once, his mother, who was a most regal looking woman, was called "Her Grace" by one of the drivers — or so I was told. At any rate, the American tourists really felt they were getting their money's worth.

One Sunday afternoon, Aileen took me to a tea party at the Bullock-Websters' — they had a beautifully kept garden behind their cottage of creosoted clapboards and cedar shakes in Oak Bay. The odd hollyhock, leaning haphazardly against the back of the house, helped to set off the trim neatness of the rockeries and the lawn and as Mrs. Bullock-Webster said, was a reminder of "home" — Major W. H. Bullock-Webster had been an English actor and was the director of the Beaux Arts plays. The ladies wore frilly, patterned summer dresses and picture hats (Aileen had a big black one on, I remember), while the men, most of them, were dressed in blazers and white or gray flannels; Henry Worthington, who had played the male lead in the last play and looked an actor with his chiselled, mobile face, wore a light summer suit. Aileen was one of the Major's leading ladies, and it was only because of her that I was there; most of the dozen or so at the garden party were connected with the Beaux Arts or the musical society, although I did see a fellow reporter, Jimmy Nesbitt, balancing a cup of tea, but he did reviews for the *Times.*

(Old George Dyke was the part-time music critic, and he was paid so much a column inch, but it was so little that it was largely a labour of love.)

As might be expected, the conversation at the Bullock-Websters' tea party had to do with the stage and its plight; the talking pictures seemed to have sounded its death knell. Then, there was the controversy over the live theatre's role, whether it should be just entertainment, or whether it shouldn't have a message, "leave you something to think about" — this was the old drawing-room-comedy-versus-social-drama argument and it had been given a new impetus by the experimental theatre in San Francisco which was being promoted by, of all things, a government agency, the WPA. Naturally, I was on the side of those who plunked for significance, the "living newspapers" of the San Francisco experiments, and I would put my two bits worth into the conversation, but I was afraid to say too much in case I should disclose my abounding ignorance of the theatre and things theatrical. Major Bullock-Webster believed in entertainment, and that there was no greater satisfaction than to provide some "poor sod", in his words, with a moment of relaxation, and in the maudlin sentiment of the times, I was inclined to agree with him.

But the devil was prompting me that sunny afternoon, and I said, "But sir, if it's only entertainment, the movies can do that better than you can." There was a pained silence in the garden; this was the kind of thing only a brash reporter would have said in such company. Even the Royal Victoria was showing movies now; the Royal's stage was big enough for the Metropolitan Opera; the only theatre left where a play could be put on was the Empire, which was a real flea pit, a crummy vaudeville house on the edge of Chinatown.

That was where the Beaux Arts staged *Private Lives,* although this may have been in 1936 (my chronology is a bit mixed-up in places). It was a magnificent example of the theatre as entertainment, of what the Major was talking about — "Noel Coward at his escapist best" — and yet I had to admit that it was well done and a lot of fun. Between acts, Aileen and I had found a sidestairs where we were undisturbed and could take turns swigging a mickey of rye (I had begun to drink and figured that the best way to impress a babe was to carry a bottle on the hip.) We sat on the hard concrete steps of the sidestairs, which were filthy and littered with crumpled paper cups and empty pop bottles, and talked about the play. I didn't think that a drawing room comedy such as this had any relevance to the social conditions of the thirties, and that the plot really strained credulity — just imagine a man meeting his former wife on her honeymoon with husband number two while he's on his honeymoon with husband number two's former wife, and effecting a reconciliation with his former wife, the first former wife, if you get that. But I agreed it was a good performance.

With that digression aside, let us return to the Bullock-Websters' garden party and the package of paprika that I threw into its midst. The Major nodded his head and admitted that the movies did provide "mass entertainment", and that there were even some things that the movies could do better than the stage. But the films were only a shadow show, and no matter what improvements were made, such as sound and now colour, they would never be any more than a shadow show, a glorified magic lantern, whereas the stage was real, it was alive, it was vital.

While most at the party would have accepted this credo, the argument continued. There were those who felt that the legitimate stage should be entertaining but should reflect the manners and morals of the times, as George Bernard Shaw's plays did, and his plays certainly had a message. But others said there wasn't any difference between Shaw and the labour hall propaganda of the WPA plays in San Francisco — you might just as well be attending a union meeting, and what could be more awful than that? As for the Russian theatre, it was nothing but soapbox oratory and waving the Red flag on stage, or so it was said. Did they really think that anyone was going to be interested in this sort of trash, twenty or thirty years from now?

But what about the live theatre? How could it be saved? Or revived? That was the nagging question and the guests at the Bullock-Websters' garden party looked gloomy — the prospects were certainly not bright. There hadn't been a touring company for some time, but then Victoria wasn't on any circuit — let's face it, it was off the beaten track. The consensus was that there was no way of beating the movies, that the professional theatre would be confined to Broadway and the West End, and that in Canada the traditions of the live theatre would be carried on by amateur groups like the Beaux Arts and the Little Theatre.

There was some murmuring against the word *amateur*, with its connotation of inferiority of effort. Most Beaux Arts members at the party preferred *volunteer* and the Major would have agreed with them; and there was no doubt that performances like *Private Lives* were really accomplished, if not professional.

60

18

No sooner had I mentioned to Benny one summer morning that I should like to have an interview with Mrs. Butchart for the farm and garden page than he picked up the phone and rang old man Butchart, who invited us to lunch, if you can beat that, because the Butcharts weren't just filthy rich like the Spencers, who owned the paper and a department store and a gold mine or two, but famous — they were what Lionel Backler called the *historic* rich who had set up their own monuments to perpetuate their names, as the Rockefellers and the Guggenheims and the Carnegies had done.

The Butchart Gardens were famous in the Pacific Northwest, if not much farther afield. They had been described in publicity handouts as among the wonders of the world, and it was certainly a wonder the way they had been cut out of an old quarry. Of course, these sunken gardens were some recompense for the damage the Butcharts had done to the countryside because the hideous crater now converted to a cavern of flowers had been made by their cement company, and one of the company's plants marred the beauty of the Malahat Drive up-island and covered the fir trees around with white dust.

By midday, when I drove the editor out in my new old Essex, it was scorching hot, and the tourists looked wilted as they traipsed through the gardens, which were such a blaze of colour they hurt the eyes — but inside it was delightfully cool. The Butcharts lived in what had become a public park, but they enjoyed attention, and their rambling house had its own privacy.

Cocktails were served in the drawing room which was strictly million-aire Hollywood down to the bowing, scraping Japanese butler in a white coat. Mrs. Butchart, a stout, middle-aged woman who was dressed in a light linen suit, complained in a soft musical voice of the heat: it would spoil the roses, she said, had Mr. Nicholas seen them for they were at their best now? Wine was served with the five-course luncheon, and I had some sauterne but Benny stuck to whisky and soda; besides the butler, a uniformed maid hovered around behind us; the china was paper thin and the silver service had a deep, much-polished shine.

Yessir, there was no doubt about the seductive quality of wealth, I thought to myself.

Afterwards, Mr. R. P. Butchart, a courtly old gent with a freshly scrubbed appearance who looked cool in his alpaca coat, showed me around the house. This was too much exercise for him, the editor said; he didn't believe in exercise and he stayed behind to talk to Mrs. Butchart. Besides a tiled swimming pool, there was a bowling alley, which seemed to occupy one whole wing of the house; also a room full of mechanical toys, walking dolls and crawling animals, miniature cars and trains, many of them made in Japan — they had been collected by Mr. Butchart on his trips abroad, and the old man liked to show off his toys.

When we returned, we sat in a glassed-in sun porch facing a beautiful formal garden; the awnings were down, but we caught the brassy edge of the sun outdoors and could hear the clip clop of the tourists as I began interviewing Mrs. Butchart. There was an electric organ in the sun porch which played records, and the next thing I knew someone behind the French doors was bawling out "Love's Old Sweet Song" to the accompaniment of the organ: it was Benny, and I had to admit that he had a fine voice. (The next day, he told Archie Wills that I was a real pro, as I had conducted the interview under "extraordinary circumstances".)

On the way back, we stopped at our place on the West Saanich road, and the editor delighted my father by praising the cherry wine he had made as a "bucolic ambrosia, the equivalent of the finest liqueurs"; after that my father called it cherry brandy. Benny spoke of the history of wine making on the island and how the loganberry had taken the place of the grape, which didn't ripen properly in the Pacific Northwest; soon he was yarning about the moonshiners and the old days when Victoria was wide open and entertained the stampeders on their way to the Klondike. In fact, Victoria outfitted the great gold rush of '98.

He also alarmed my mother, not by the stories he told, but because he was so engrossed in telling them that he didn't pay any attention to his cigar; he put the wrong end in his mouth. There was a muted cry in our cedar-panelled living room, but it came from my mother: the editor merely withdrew the offending weed, turned it around and put it back in his mouth. The cigar was not lighted.

19

My old college pal, Shep McMurtry, visited Victoria that summer, as he had done, come to think of it, the previous summer, only this second visit was the more memorable. He had a second trip by "Chink train" across the continent, which meant that he must have kept his nose clean the first time and not fallen asleep on shift as I had done; when he got to Vancouver, he teamed up with Dick Harbert, a classmate at McGill, who had come out by bus. They stayed in the YMCA in Victoria for a time, and then lived in nautical style on a cousin's power cruiser, which was moored off the Yacht Club in Cadboro Bay.

A. (for Arthur) Shepherd McMurtry was named after his mother's family, the Shepherds of Como, Quebec; his great grandfather, the first Robert W. Shepherd, had started the Ottawa Navigation Company and had married the daughter of Peter Francis Christian de les Derniers, a Swiss pioneer, who had a large farm on the shore of the Lake of the Two Mountains and who was supposed to have named it Como because the lake reminded him of Lake Como.* Most of the old families like Shep's never spoke French although they had been in Montreal for generations, but Shep himself was an exception. He was taking law and felt that it was necessary to know French, and so he went to a French camp in deepest Quebec for part of one summer.

It was rather a grim experience, he told us. At the time, there was a gulf separating the two language groups in Quebec which could be measured in hundreds of years, and Shep found that he had nothing in common with any of the French Canadians at the camp. There was one weedy youth, a sallow, bony guy, with whom he could crack jokes and blaspheme a bit, but he turned out to be the black sheep of the camp, having been expelled from a seminary for immoral behavior. Then there was the fact that the fellows in his cabin never undressed fully; they would always leave their underwear on. That got him down because it made him feel like a peeping Tom or an exhibitionist. Shep's explanation was that they had been brought up never to expose themselves before anyone, even members of their own sex, as this was regarded as a sin by the Roman Catholic Church.

*Another case where nostalgia eliminated a better "original" name — Cavagnal.

"You don't say," I said. Frankly I was astonished; I had gone swimming with Sunny Gilroy and a priest who was a friend of his and they never behaved in this extraordinary manner. Later when I told Gil about it, he explained that the Catholic Church varied a lot and the one in Quebec was very primitive.

Once aboard the boat, Shep and Dick Harbert kept a weather eye out for Cadborosaurus,* the sea monster that so many Victorians had seen gallumphing around Cadboro Bay and out in the open straits, but without any luck. (After the sightings became so frequent that they were no longer news, they developed into an occasional feature in a gossip column that Tom Merriman had in the weekend section of the *Victoria Times*.) The boys even drank several bottles of beer, all in the interest of research, of course, and squinted into the dazzle that the late afternoon sun made on the water — this was said to be the best way and best time to spot Caddy — but they saw not a hair of this shaggy creature of the deep. All they got for their scientific endeavours was a headache.

We did use the boat to cruise around the coast beyond Ten Mile Point and Gordon Head and anchor off some islet where there were flat rocks on which to warm up after a chilling plunge into the dark sea; sometimes the rocks were too hot and we would stretch out on the driftwood that festooned these islets and had been pounded satin smooth by winter storms. Those were the days, all right, and we lay there soaking up the salt and the ozone and the sunshine, on the broad rippling bosom of the Strait of Juan de Fuca. We might have been the only living souls around, for the boat and the houses of Victoria were hidden from our view, and there was nothing to be seen but the empty sea and the primaeval forests, the eternal fir trees rising from the shore.

Shep swore that he'd move to Vancouver Island and become a lotus eater like the rest of us, but his family had been too long in Montreal, and had too many interests there, and the only reason he had come out to the Pacific Coast two summers running was that he couldn't get a part-time job. This was the summer of 1935, remember.

There was one incident that I would like to draw attention to, as it showed how small-minded the babes in Victoria were. When we went to a Saturday night dance at the Empress Hotel, Dick Harbert brought along his recorder, on which he could tootle quite tunefully; he entertained the assembled company during one intermission, and there was a round of appreciative applause. But not from the babes we had provided Shep and Dick. They told me later that it was a disgraceful performance, that they had been publicly humiliated, and for crying out loud, they

*Archie Wills first publicized Victoria's sea monster in 1933.

64

blamed me. I needn't tell you those dames got a pretty low rating in my little black book.

As a farewell party for Shep, who had stayed on after Dick Harbert left, we planned a monumental bash at Jack Trace's place on Glen Lake, starting in the afternoon and going on all night. The girls looked after the food, and Aileen organized it so that they didn't all bring potato salad, and it must be said in defence of the Island females that they did do things like that, that they were unspoiled if hopelessly inhibited (witness the row over Dick's tootling), a condition possibly unique in the North American experience. Mind you, as Lionel Backler would have pointed out, there was the sociological fact that there were more girls than boys in Victoria, since many of the fellows had to leave "this other Eden, demi-paradise," to earn a living.

Jack Trace was an amiable, easygoing friend who had the use of his family's cottage at Glen Lake on the odd weekend; the cottage was on the opposite side of the lake from the road and had to be reached by walking down a railroad track. We had to make several journeys to move all the booze and provender from the cars to the cottage, and the track was burning hot in the blazing sunshine; we were sweltering and the sight of the lake shimmering through the pine trees was cool and inviting; we tore off the pants we had on over our bathing suits and rushed down the bank, across the rickety wooden pier, and splashed into the water. The girls came tripping down some half-hour later, or so it seemed, giggling and stuffing their hair under their rubber caps.

It was drinking time when the shadows had obscured the Trace's raft, which was almost halfway across the small lake. As this was a special occasion, we had brought, besides beer, a couple of crocks, and Dick Hoyle, who had had some experience as a bartender, was mixing what he called "the only, genuine, original tiger's milk". This was like dynamite and blasted the party off to a quick start. Superlatives were shouted: the drink was marvellous, scrumptious (or was that the food?), colossal, terrific, the bestest, "the only, genuine, original tiger's milk". A portable gramophone, which had been lugged over the hot track, was playing loudly and tinnily, "Dancing Cheek to Cheek", and "Begin the Beguine". The noise had reached such a level in the confined quarters of the cabin that I couldn't hear what Shep was saying, but I gathered that he was enjoying himself. So was everyone else.

One of the girls climbed a tree, almost to the top, then panicked and couldn't get down; so, an expedition had to be organized to rescue her. By the time the party ended and people were packing up their bits and pieces in the gray dawn, I was so lightheaded that I thought it was screamingly funny when someone said: "I figured it was passion at last, but she was only being sick."

20

On August 24, 1935 the *Victoria Daily Times* should have devoted the eight-column headline that it used for the main story of the day to the stunning victory of the Social Credit Party in the Alberta election which had been held two days before, but Bill Henderson was in a dither and failed to grasp the significance of this event: the first political upheaval of the great depression. At any rate, looking through the yellowing files, I came upon the historic report under what must have been the most insipid two column heading that the telegraph editor was able to devise:

NEW PARTY GAINS
SEATS IN ALBERTA

A few days later, it was announced that the leader of this new party, William Aberhart, had become the province's premier. Old Bible Bill — from the pulpit of the Prophetic Bible Institute in Calgary and over the radio, he had spread the gospel according to Major Douglas with its funny money creed, and had brought down the wrath of the common people on the old parties, the Conservatives and the Liberals and the newer United Farmers, so that they were destroyed and would never rise again, not in his time, nor in the time of his successor, Ernest Manning. Social Credit swept the province, and the damnedest bunch of people with straw in their hair descended on the provincial capital of Edmonton: at their head was this fat, pallid schoolteacher-cum-evangelist-prophet, but at least Bible Bill believed the monetary mumbo jumbo. He tried to take over the banks, the poor sap, but the Eastern financiers and their servants in Ottawa put a stop to that.

However, he did issue his own money, the depression dollar, a revolving buck which had to have a two cent stamp stuck on it every time it was passed, a tatterdemalion piece of currency, which was always being repaired with bits of sticky paper to prevent it from falling apart before it was fully covered with stamps and could be redeemed for a real buck. The disintegrating dollar.

On September 9, 1935 the teletype machine in the CP office behind the telegraph desk clattered out the news that Senator Huey P. Long had been fatally wounded. He had been shot the night before in the marble corridors of the skyscraper State House that he had built in the

Louisiana capital and which would be his monument. His assailant was a young doctor, Carl Austin Weiss, whose father was a political opponent of the Kingfish, but Weiss' motives were never known for he was killed immediately, riddled with more than sixty bullets fired by Huey Long's panic-stricken bodyguards. When he got the bulletin, Bill Henderson went around cursing, which was his way of expressing astonishment. Even Lionel Backler was amazed, and he recalled that we had heard Huey Long on the air just a short time before. But Lionel, who had warned that the Kingfish was a fascist and might become the American dictator, was now suggesting that FDR might have had a hand in his assassination — it certainly cleared the way for Roosevelt in '36. He was trying to get a rise out of Benny, who had come into the news room, a large unlit cigar sticking out of his cherubic face, but the editor glanced at the copy and waddled out without being drawn into the discussion. We were excited at the news and figured the full story would make fascinating reading, but it was never told. After news of his death, and he died the next day in good time for the evening papers, there was no more about Huey P. Long.

That fall, Canada was in the toils of a general election campaign, and the papers were full of domestic politics. Prime Minister Bennett had hung on as long as he could, always hoping for the "happy days around the corner", but after five years in office, he had to go to the country. There was no longer the threat of an unemployed march on Ottawa; he had stopped the relief camp strikers and turned them back at Regina. Yet, it was a hollow victory, and his main opponent, former prime minister Mackenzie King, would make the most of it on the hustings, although there was no doubt that if the opposition leader had been in power, he would have done the same, and sicked the RCMP onto the strikers in Regina. It was a case of tweedledum and tweedledee, and the two portly leaders of the Conservative and Liberal parties looked the part. The *Victoria Daily Times* was beating the drum for the Liberals. As an election was in the offing — it was called for mid-October — the paper reverted to what it was when the Honourable William Templeman, the sometime Laurier minister, had founded it as a party sheet. The eight column banner headlines became party slogans:

LIBERALS PLAN WIDE RECONSTRUCTION
KING DECLARED ONLY FREE LEADER
CO-OPERATION IS SLOGAN OF LIBERALS

It was really advertising, that's what it was, and the *Times* was being used as a flyer to plug the Liberal brand of politics as opposed to the Conservative brand, which was being touted by the *Colonist*, the morning paper down the street. And they were about as different as two brands of soap flakes.

A new force had appeared, however, in the shape of King Gordon, who was running in Victoria for the new Socialist party, which had such a ghastly name that only the initials, CCF, were used (standing for the Co-operative Commonwealth Federation, whatever that meant). He was young, good-looking, energetic, with an aura of martyrdom about him, for as a divinity professor, he had been bounced from McGill University because of his leftist views. Furthermore, he came from a prominent western family; his father was a well-known Canadian author who wrote under the name of Ralph Connor. Still, the existence of a Red (even a Pinko) among the lotus eaters, as Bruce Hutchison called the denizens of Vancouver Island, was very disturbing.

Perhaps because he was a novelty, King Gordon was drawing the crowds, two hundred and fifty in the Grain Exchange Hall on View Street, more than three hundred at the Shrine Auditorium, whereas the local Liberal meetings averaged twenty-five or thirty bored ward heelers. He was a political phenomenon, all right.

Archie Wills considered him the biggest news maker in Victoria during the election campaign, and he said so to Benny when he argued with the editor that there should be equal treatment for all political parties on the news pages. He spoke of the crowds that the CCF candidate was drawing. Oh, he admitted that the leaders drew large crowds, but the ordinary Tory or Grit candidate couldn't fill a telephone booth. There was a big turnout for R. B. Bennett. The seventeen hundred seats in the Royal Victoria Theatre were filled when the Prime Minister spoke and hundreds milled around outside, not all of them friendly, but they were interested. It was at this meeting that the Conservative leader had defended the actions he had taken to stop the relief camp strikers' march on Ottawa.

"The object of that march was to hold the prime minister as hostage and set up a Soviet at Ottawa," he bellowed at the serried ranks of well-dressed citizens, whose fears and expectations he was confirming. He was also confirming Lionel Backler's view that the march on Ottawa was a revolutionary movement, although Lionel scoffed at this and at the "heroics" of the old reactionary.

When Mackenzie King visited the island a week later, he also drew a packed house at the Royal Victoria. His was a typically dull speech about trade and the necessity for its revival; it had no fascinating revelations about Red revolution, but it rated an eight column headline with a drop about the "enthusiastic reception" of the great "friendly" audience, whereas Mr. Bennett's speech was dismissed with a two column heading, which did, however, deal with his communist nightmare. The fact that Mackenzie King's meeting had Ben Nicholas as chairman might have had something to do with the better play it received; then, there was the long-drawn-out agony of Western indecision over fascist Italy's impending attack on the defenceless black kingdom of Ethiopia, and the streamer on the day the paper carried the report on Prime Minister Bennett's awful "kidnapping" disclosure was:

LEAGUE'S ETHIOPIA COMMITTEE FAILS

When Archie Wills argued with the editor for equal treatment of the political parties on the news pages, he was not pleading for fair play or anything like that; although he was the soul of integrity, a non-drinking, non-smoking, churchgoer in the licentious city room, he was an out-and-out Liberal partisan. It was as a newspaperman that he was offended by the spread given Mackenzie King, whose meeting was as dull as ditchwater and had none of R. B. Bennett's Red scare, and by the way in which King Gordon's socialist evangelism was being ignored.

Yet he had a hard time convincing Ben Nicholas. When he raised the question of the election coverage, Archie squirmed around in his hard wooden chair while the editor wondered aloud whether the Tories expected a fair break from a Liberal paper; certainly, the Grits didn't get one in the *Colonist*. It was during the morning conference in the editor's dingy office, and Benny was expatiating as he usually did, sitting forward in his chair, his stomach resting on his legs, chomping on a cigar and every now and then spitting a loosened leaf into the brass spittoon, which was in perfect range from his swivel chair. Archie Wills himself reported on the conversation some time later, and the news editor was a reliable witness as he kept a diary.

If we reported King Gordon's meetings, Mr. Nicholas said, we would be spoiling the socialist case in the election campaign, and we wouldn't want to do that, would we? The CCF'ers wouldn't be able to go around blaming everything on the lying capitalist press, and that would be bad for them, wouldn't it? The editor had a quizzical look on his great moon face as he warmed to the subject and expectorated a bit of the chewed up cigar, which landed with a neat plop, dead centre. There was nothing wrong with good honest-to-gosh partisanship, he went on, you knew where a paper stood then, but nowadays, that namby-pamby seeing-things-from-every-point-of-view approach would produce nothing but a dull, gray sheet — and already this was happening, and the editor let out a sigh and looked at the portrait of William Templeman as though seeking advice. It was a great act.

Although Archie Wills was not entirely successful, he did get Ben Nicholas to agree that the reports from the hustings should be treated in the same way as other news. It was an agreement in principle, broken often in practice, but the *Victoria Times'* election coverage was about as fair as could be expected in the thirties. Archie was proud of it and he was delighted when King Gordon made a point of thanking him for the objective reporting of his meetings. However, the news editor could not stop the Liberals from being on the front page when all the other parties were relegated to inside the paper.

Still, the Grits were denied the streamer which was occupied almost daily with the beginning of the Ethiopian War:

October 4, ITALIANS DRIVE ON INTO ETHIOPIA;
October 5, ETHIOPIA ASKS LEAGUE MILITARY MOVES;
October 7, LEAGUE'S VOTE TODAY AGAINST ITALY.

Such world-shaking news obscured the party puffs, and Mackenzie King's assurance that there would be no rail merger if and when the Liberals came to power, and his denunciation of Conservative promises were on the front page but under two column headings.

The trouble with the 1935 election was that it was a foregone conclusion. The Conservative government of Prime Minister R. B. Bennett had been smashed by the great depression and had disintegrated, with Harry Stevens, a former Bennett cabinet minister, breaking away and forming his own so-called Reconstruction Party. All the powerful forces that had pushed the Tories into power had swung behind the Liberals, for "revolution was haunting the land", or the western part of it, although it was a forelorn ghost in the shape of the CCF.

For a moment during the election campaign, the mob claimed the hustings. That was at the Bennett meeting in Vancouver. There were many unemployed and relief camp strikers in the great jam-packed hockey arena, and they had come to boo the Prime Minister, not to hear him. It was a frightening noise, the clamour of the angry crowd, but Bennett would not be subdued; he grabbed the public address mike and shouted above the uproar: "You thugs, you hoodlums — is this your idea of democracy?" The bellowing, whistling storm drowned out his words, but he would not go down, this portly man in black coat and striped pants, the very caricature of a bloated capitalist, but a man of guts who would not bow before the rabble, even before the guillotine. His performance that night should have won him friends and supporters, and would have if they hadn't already put their money on Mackenzie King. After an hour, the tide of fury began to ebb. "What a cowardly lot," Bennett said as his tormentors began to leave, two or three here, then hundreds there, until solid blocks of seats had been emptied. By the time he was able to resume his speech, half of his audience had gone.

On the night of October 8, the Liberals put on a broadcast that was an election blockbuster. They lined up the premiers of eight of the nine provinces in their provincial capitals, strung them together with thousands of miles of wire, and got them to speak on behalf of the federal party over a nation-wide radio hookup. EIGHT CANADIAN PREMIERS BACKING LIBERAL POLICY, said the *Times* streamer headline, and all were Liberals, although Premier John Bracken of Manitoba, who called himself a Liberal Progressive then, was to become Conservative Party leader, changing the party's name to Progressive Conservative. (The ninth premier was Bible Bill Aberhart of Alberta.) It was a demonstration of the overwhelming force behind the Liberals.

During the week before the election, Archie Wills had made an unusual request of the editor, that the *Times* hire a public address system and broadcast the results of the election to the crowd that would gather on the corner of Fort and View streets; this would take the place of putting up the bulletins in the ground floor windows, which had been done every election. The cost would be seventy-five dollars. Benny grumbled about the amount involved, and gloomily forecast that there would be a downpour on election night, but agreed. On October 14, polling day, the editor put his head out of the window and said there was a lot of "gas" out there, which was his way of proclaiming the presence of clouds and the possibility of a storm. However, the rain held off, and the *Times* election "broadcast" was a great success. All of which might have been due to habit dying hard, the fact that Victorians had always come down to the papers on election night to find out the results, but the big crowd on October 14, 1935 was also a sign that radio had not yet arrived as a news medium, although it was on the way.

Ted Fox, the police reporter and the younger of the Foxes on the paper — his brother, Les, covered the legislature — was picked to do the announcing, as he had a resonant voice and had a reputation as an M.C. He did his best to make it sound exciting, although the difference in the time zones meant that the contest had been decided before the polls closed on the Pacific Coast and we were allowed to give out the results. D. B. Plunkett, who held Victoria for the Conservatives, visited the news room during the night; so did King Gordon, whom Plunkett had beaten by less than a thousand votes, with the Liberal candidate a close third.

Across the country, the Liberals steamrollered the opposition; they won 171 seats to the Conservatives 39, but in the far West, it was different: the Social Credit cohorts of Bible Bill Aberhart took 15 of the 17 seats in Alberta and another 2 in Saskatchewan, while in British Columbia, there was a more even split, with the Liberals winning 6, the

Conservatives 5, the CCF 3 (7 in the whole of Canada), and Harry Steven's Reconstruction Party only 1 seat, which was his own.

After that, except for the swearing in of Prime Minister Mackenzie King's new government, which was strictly a non-news event but which the *Victoria Daily Times* dutifully splashed, there was no more domestic politics in the papers.

21

As a result of the 1935 election, the papers became less political pamphlets and more newspapers. While Mr. Nicholas had seemed reluctant to allow this to occur at the time, he agreed that it was progress and a proper development. Perhaps it was due to his close association with the founder of the *Times,* the Honourable William Templeman, but Benny did point out that most papers in Canada had been started by political parties, or been financed by them; and as he said, while a free press was a guarantee of political freedoms, the reverse could be said: that by starting the papers, the freedom of the press had been guaranteed by the political parties.

Victoria was a classic example of what Ben Nicholas was talking about. The *Daily Colonist* had been started by an extraordinary eccentric and Tory, Amor De Cosmos, who like his opposite number on the *Times* (only Templeman was much later) went to Ottawa as an MP, although his career in provincial politics was more noteworthy.*

A portrait painting of Amor De Cosmos hung in the *Colonist* office: a man with a jet-black beard, old Bluebeard himself, in a Prince Albert and come-to-Jesus collar, a hot-tempered, aggressive little fellow, who would pick fights with the town's leading citizens on the streets, a demagogue, a free thinker, a vainglorious bachelor, a man of vision, who campaigned for the union of the colonies of Vancouver Island and British Columbia and was a leader in the struggle for confederation and responsible government. (No wonder Pinkie McKelvie was fired. He wanted to reverse what the founder had fought for and won.)

De Cosmos and another newspaperman, Sam McClure, set a filibustering record in the old British Columbia Legislature, the Bird Cage as it was called: they talked for twenty-four hours. De Cosmos spoke for seven hours without sitting down. According to an account of the time; "His voice, never the most musical, had sunk into a mere squeak, like that emitted by a half-drowned rat, and he appeared at times scarcely able to stand. On the table beside him was a tumblerful of eggnog from which he occasionally imbibed."

*Hon. Amor De Cosmos, Premier of British Columbia, December, 1872 to February, 1874.

Although all this occurred half a century before, Benny talked of Amor De Cosmos as though he were an old friend, or a patron who had passed away only yesterday like the Honourable William Templeman. He never failed to mention the fact that Amor De Cosmos's real name was Bill Smith and that he had his name changed by act of the California Legislature during the gold rush of forty-nine. The chuckles would start at the editor's eyes and go shaking down his egg-shaped body until they were lost amid the folds of his suit around his belly. Amor De Cosmos, he would say, waving his unlighted cigar, was proof positive that a name made the man, and not the man the name. All that stuff about a rose by any other name being just as sweet was all bullshit. Bill Smith would have got nowhere, but Amor De Cosmos . . . and did anybody know how he got that name? Well, he made it up. Amor De Cosmos meant Lover of the World, and the editor collapsed in a convulsive flood of mirth.

1936

22

At the end of January, 1936, Rudyard Kipling and King George V died within a couple of days of each other; they were of the same age, the "venerable" monarch, as the agency copy described the King, was only seventy. Kipling's death astonished most of us, and Bill Henderson expressed our surprise when he said while calling on Anaemic Jesus as a witness, that he thought the poet of the Empire had died during the Indian Mutiny. It was easy to say that the King's death marked the end of an era, as the editor did in a black-bordered leader which included every cliché and ended: "The King is dead — Long Live the King."

It was the end of something. George V, the Sailor King, who might have been a mean old bastard for all I knew, but looked like an Emperor, was being succeeded by Edward VIII, the Prince Charming (no greater honour could be paid anyone than that a car be named after him — the Windsor White Prince) who was destined to let the whole side down before the year was ended.

There were other changes too, and the news room would not be the same for me now that Lionel Backler had left. He had talked about going from the moment that I had met him, saying that you couldn't stay in Victoria if you expected to get anywhere — there was no future, just a comfortable present — and he agreed with Bruce Hutchison, which must have been the only time he did, that this was a land of lotus eaters. Lionel had met the son of a New York publisher when he was at UBC, and this fellow who wasn't much older than himself, had inherited the whole kit and kaboodle when his father died and was going to start a magazine because that would be his fulfillment, and he was goddamn concerned about his fulfillment. At any rate, Lionel was going to work on the magazine — mind you, I never did know whether he had a job or not, but he left the *Victoria Daily Times* and went to New York. Lionel would have jeered at that black-bordered editorial on the King's death, and I felt depressed.

On the next day or the day after, I felt better because the editor was in a good mood; when I brought in the galley proof of an interview I had with a visiting evangelist, Benny was putting on his favourite act. "You cheap, chiselling bastard," he was bawling into the telephone, which was perched atop a pile of papers on his roll-top desk — I couldn't tell whether it was the long suffering Premier Pattullo* at the end of the line, but that was the editor's usual manner of addressing any member of the Liberal government of British Columbia.

There was no doubt that Ben Nicholas had a guilty conscience about politicians; he was one of them and when an election was called, he was as good a party man as any of them, but he seemed to feel that this was somehow wrong, and so, by various means, some of them pretty devious, he would attack the Liberal Party and its program in his paper. Such an editorial blast would be carefully timed to do no harm, but it would cause alarm and despondency among his Liberal friends, which would delight him. In the same way, he would take it out on the politicians; he would keep them waiting, and on one occasion, he sneaked out of the back door of his office, leaving the Minister of Education, a professor turned politician, squirming on a hard wooden chair in his anteroom. From assuaging his conscience by insulting politicians, Benny developed the habit of being rude and boorish to the mighty and elaborately courteous and considerate to the humble; he would treat Joe, the north country English janitor, as if he were a diplomat.

I put the galley proof on his garbage heap of a desk and the editor glanced at it while delivering his favourite homily on the freedom of the press. Evidently, the caller had complained about Bruce Hutchison's column, and Mr. Nicholas was elaborately defending himself; he said that he couldn't interfere in any way, that to expunge or alter a word in a columnist's copy would be censorship, which was the worst crime in the annals of journalism. His voice rose in a crescendo of indignation, and at the same time, he gave me a broad wink.

Everyone in the office knew that he had started Bruce Hutchison writing "Loose Ends" when the Liberals came to power in British Columbia in 1933 so that he would have a vehicle for attacking the provincial government — it would have been awkward for him to do so through the editorial columns, as the *Victoria Times* was subsidized by the Liberal Party. Everyone knew that he provided Bruce with much of his ammunition. Old Benny had been pretty cute about this, but surely he didn't think that nobody outside the paper knew of it. Meanwhile he read my story while the bigshot politician, whoever he was, poured his grievance into a half-attentive ear.

A broad grin lit up his smooth fish face as he returned to the telephone, and it was as if he were going to swallow the upright receiver. If the caller would stop his "whining" for a moment, the editor said, he had some news for him. Did he realize that Victoria had been visited by a

*Hon. Thomas Dufferin Pattullo, premier of British Columbia, 1933–1941.

missionary, and a Christian missionary, who had been interviewed by one of the paper's best young reporters — and Benny gave me another broad wink and a chuckle rippled silently down his vest.

Did he realize that it was because of the government's wickedness that the missionary had come here. And what did the missionary say, the editor went on, but that the people were sinful and had turned from the path of righteousness (he was reading from my report) and that they were looking for guidance — a guidance, Benny added, that they wouldn't get from the corrupt government of British Columbia.

Mr. Nicholas read from the galley proof that the evangelist wanted to start a temple for Aimee Semple McPherson in Victoria, and what did the government think of that? — wasn't it opposed to the way that the Pacific Coast was being turned into a lunatic fringe? There was more in the same vein. At last, the telephone conversation ended, and with a whoop the editor hung up; he wiped his face with his pudgy hand and chortled.

The first edition was delivered by the office boy, and after thanking him profusely, Benny signalled me to stay while he glanced through the paper. The front page was full of the preparations for the funeral of King George V, but under the banner headline was a two column picture of Emperor Haile Selassie of Ethiopia, seated before a microphone with a white man in a tuxedo standing behind him. The caption read that the first thing that Joseph Israels, the New York press agent who had been hired by the Ethiopian government, had done was to get the Emperor to use the modern facilities of radio.

It was a bit late for a publicity man, the editor said with a snort. Haile Selassie would be better off with what Benny described as "my holy roller friend" or one of his own witch doctors because he needed a real earth-shaking miracle right now. Musso's blackshirts had conquered most of the country.

Still, radio had made a big difference, Ben Nicholas mused, communications were so much better than when he was a marine reporter and covered Asian affairs by rewriting the papers on the Pacific liners. Chang Tso-lin and Wu Pei-fu were very great Chinese war lords, he said, and they commanded hosts of hundreds of thousands of men and they won and lost, mostly they lost — but who the hell had ever heard of them? As far as old Haile Selassie was concerned, though, radio would mean that we would know about the fall of Addis Ababa here in Victoria, B.C., only moments after the Italian Fascists entered the Ethiopian capital.

The bain of Benny's life was a certain Miss Dora Kitto, a worthy woman of uncertain age, who bombarded him with letters to the editor about cruelty to animals and the horrors of vivisection. The case at issue didn't have to have occurred in Victoria (in fact, it seldom did) to arouse her irate pen, and woe betide the editor if he ignored the letter or consigned it to the editorial wastepaper basket, for he would be visited by Miss Kitto in person, waving a large umbrella as if it were a battle-axe. One afternoon after the last deadline, Mr. Nicholas wondered aloud how he could control this formidable female and he hit on the idea that I should write a letter, under a nom de plume, about cruelty to vegetables.

In due course, a letter by "Vegetable Lover" appeared on the editorial page of the *Times;* it started off by praising the work of the local anti-vivisection society and the SPCA, but said "the vegetable world calls them with tearful entreaty". Then it offered the information that "one famous British scientist", unnamed, had declared that plants suffered the same as animals or human beings do, although his fellow scientists didn't agree. But how did they know? the letter asked and went on to say:

> We are assuming something which may be entirely false, and our assumption leads us to perform the most frightful tortures. Think of the exquisite agony rhubarb must suffer when it is cut up on the kitchen table — worse by far than the Oriental torture of a thousand knives.
>
> Then the wretched carrot wrenched from the warmth of mother earth to be skinned alive — the cabbage grown to youthful beauty to have its limbs torn off — unripe pea pods ruthlessly disemboweled by the housewives' thumb — these are but a few examples of man's inhumanity to plants.
>
> Think also of the many little green things we torture less obviously — the grass we trample under foot — the trees upon whose skin we carve our initials — the beets we squeeze to death for sugar.
>
> Perhaps the worst aspect of our torture of plant life is the way we pick flowers. We tear up these beautiful ornaments of nature to allow them to die a lingering death indoors. We feed them water so that they may die more slowly. And why do we do it? Not because of gnawing hunger but merely because of vanity.

The letter ended by announcing the formation of a Society for the Promotion of Kindliness to Plant Life. There was a good deal of Mr. Nicholas in that letter,* as we had talked over its contents in detail, but I don't think he wrote any part of it; at any rate, the editor was delighted and amused, and the letter seemed to have the desired effect, since there was nothing from Miss Kitto in the paper for some weeks.

*Some time before I joined the paper, Mr. Nicholas had written a letter to the editor under the pseudonym of L. Puller (first name Leg), saying he had seen a Zipple. Of course, there is no such thing, but it was amazing the number of people who claimed also to have seen one.

23

It was on a mild February day, if my memory serves me right, that a representative group of the *Times* editorial staff trooped down to the old courthouse area of Victoria to join the British Public School Boys' Club. There was a promise of spring in the soft sunshine, the first daffodils were blooming — it was the sort of day that Vancouver Islanders wrote about, and still write about, in letters to their less fortunate fellow Canadians. A fistful of blank membership cards for the club, which was under new management, had been received by the news desk that morning, and Archie Wills distributed them to members of the staff; most accepted with a wild derisory whoop, but the news editor didn't avail himself of the invitation.

Among the merry band that set forth after the last edition had gone to press was Pete Sallaway, the sports editor, who looked like a news hawk with his big beak of a nose; when he arrived for work in the morning, and he was the first in the news room as the sports pages were locked up earlier than other news pages, he would take off his coat and take out his false teeth, placing the latter on his desk with the front facing him and grinning at him as he batted out his graphic but ungrammatical copy on his beat-up typewriter. The sight of the store teeth in all their naked nastiness offended Nancy Hodges, the society editor, whose desk was just across the way from Pete's; she considered this dental display to be "coarse" and "vulgar" and said so, but her protest had no other effect than to produce a rather coarse and vulgar reply from the sports editor, who could enunciate just as clearly, with or without his teeth.

Nancy Hodges was a formidable Englishwoman of commanding presence, who was to have a most distinguished political career; she was active in women's organizations and was to become president of the National Federation of Liberal Women; she ran in the provincial general election of 1937 and didn't make it then, but after I had left the *Victoria Times*, was elected; when she was named Speaker of the British Columbia Legislature it was the first time that a woman had attained this high parliamentary office in the history of the Commonwealth. Later, when the whole applecart of the Liberal Conservative coalition government was upset (by Social Credit), Nancy received her just reward from a grateful party and was "summoned" to the Canadian Senate.

Her husband, Harry Hodges, was an associate editor and editorial writer at the time and had an office on the floor below. He was a plump west country Englishman, who had a remarkably strong constitution; the Hodges came to Canada before the First World War, and shortly thereafter, Harry came down with galloping consumption, as it was called then, and given up for dead at Tranquille TB Sanitarium in British Columbia, but recovered from that; he now appeared to be drinking himself to death, but survived to accompany his wife to Ottawa and attain a ripe old age.

Les and Ted Fox were in the group that made its way down Fort Street to the club, and so was Tom Merriman, who helped Archie out on the news desk and wrote a weekly gossip column. Tom was a smaller version of the editor, a round roly-poly man; he was the only member of the staff who was shorter than Benny and he stood behind the editor in the 1934 anniversary photograph that was taken of the editorial staff lined up according to height — this was the picture with Lionel Backler, 6 ft. 7 ins., first, Peter Inglis, 6 ft. 5 ins., second, myself a poor third, with the Canadian Press man, Graham Harris, and Pete Sallaway next. Why Mr. Nicholas should have led this raffish expedition was explained by the editor's sense of humour: here was the club to which the élite belonged (the sons of the wealthy Englishmen in Victoria had been sent to British Public Schools), taken over by "Joker" Patton, the town's leading bootlegger, who had been able to retain the club's name as a condition of purchasing the license. Old Benny chortled as he waddled down the street.

I can't remember whether Peter Inglis was with us on this occasion. He had inherited his job on the *Victoria Daily Times*, or so it was said, as his father, who had been city editor of the paper, marched off to the First World War and was killed at Cambrai. His picture hung in the anteroom to the editor's office. Mr. Nicholas was Peter's godfather and had been a good and generous friend — rumour had it that he had paid for his godson's education at Cheltenham, the British public school, for Peter was brought up in the old country (his mother was English and had met and married Tommy Inglis overseas during the war). Peter had a ripe English accent, which was not remarkable in Victoria where so many had English accents, even some who had never been off Vancouver Island.

The other members of the editorial staff at the time were Ken Drury, the feature editor; Dick Freeman, a quiet, bald-headed rewrite man; Art Stott, who had been quite an athlete in his day; Jimmy Nesbitt

Irving Strickland; Cap Thorsen, the office boy; and of course, Bill Henderson, the telegraph editor, and Bruce Hutchison, the columnist, who did most of his work at home in Saanich and only came to the office to deliver his copy and pick up his mail. It was not a large editorial staff, and we comfortably filled that anniversary picture,* but the *Victoria Times'* circulation was just over ten thousand then.

The British Public School Boys' Club was around the corner from the courthouse in one of the more substantial stone buildings. A brass plate beside the door was engraved with the club's name in old English script: inside was a dark entrance hall with rows of coat hooks, which led into a high-ceilinged room: at one end was a baronial fire place, and off one side, what had been a panelled reading room and library; cheap metal chairs and tables now filled both rooms, the French doors dividing the two having been taken down.

By acquiring the British Public School Boys' license, Joker Patton had become the proprietor of the sort of phony club that was nothing more than a bar which the province's ludicrous liquor laws allowed; he had a legitimate business enterprise now, which, as he admitted, was a lot less worry than bootlegging, although that wasn't so risky if you knew what to do — like anything else, he added with a knowing wink.

A cross section of Victoria's drinking public (male) was at the opening, and there was loud talk in affected English accents of schools and school ties and such like. Derisory cries of so-and-so's an Old Bastard, or an Old Reprobate, or an Old Bullshitter, greeted us as we entered the premises. The Joker found us a table; he was delighted that Benny Nicholas should have come and he sought to assure the editor that the club would continue to be a respectable, high-class joint, with all the fine old British tradition, whatever that was, preserved; the only thing he would add was some honest bookkeeping.

Rebel Mowat was at the table next to us; he was still in his spieler's uniform, and had just come from conducting a bus load of American tourists to the Butchart Gardens. Besides being the best goddamned tourist guide in the whole Pacific Northwest, as everyone said, and the greatest booster Victoria had ever had, Rebel was the town clown: he had a comic baseball team known as Cox's Army, which drew huge crowds to the sports grounds, especially when famous sports personalities joined its ranks. Now he was looking quizzically at the editor, apparently astonished to see him at such a rapscallion event, his peak cap at the back of his head, his eyes glinting in his pudgy boxer's face.

*Also in the picture were Cornelius F. "Mory" Moriarty of Canadian Press, Frank Pagett from the Saanich council beat, and Mrs. H. A. Whillans, who wrote for the Society page.

When the drinks were delivered at our table, Rebel held up a warning hand. Didn't we know that they were from the old stock? he asked, in his husky Brooklyn Irish voice. Hadn't the Joker told us? Them limies might have poisoned the hooch. Here, he said, he would sample the first drink — it was because of the high esteem that he had for the editor that he was providing this service.

And Rebel picked up a glass of rye and tossed it back. As he did so, a shudder shook his ample frame, he stiffened and gripped the side of our table. His rubber ball of a face seemed to be exploding, his eyes popping out. The hissing, gurgling sound coming from him turned to throat-rattling gasps. His limbs became disjointed. He let go of the table and started to jerk and totter. Then, after a couple of quavering recoveries, he collapsed and lay prone on the floor, his tongue out, the glass in one hand balanced nicely on his chest.

It was a staggering performance, and there was a generous burst of laughter and applause, although many had seen him put on this act before. I had seen him do it when he was showing some American ladies around Hatley Park, one of the Dunsmuir estates, which has become Royal Roads naval college; two of the well-dressed club women wondered if it were safe to drink the water from a garden tap, and Rebel said that he would test it for them, and then collapsed on the garden path as he had collapsed on the bar room floor.

Benjamin Charles Nicholas, editor of the *Victoria Daily Times*. (*Courtesy BC Archives and Records Service*)

The *Victoria Daily Times* Building, at the corner of Fort and Broad streets. (*Courtesy City of Victoria Archives*)

A group of Native Sons of B. C., *ca* 1935. Bruce McKelvie, (back row, sixth from right) was for many years the Grand Factor of this order. (*Courtesy City of Victoria Archives*)

Mrs. R. P. Butchart, founder of the Butchart Gardens, *ca* 1926. (*Courtesy City of Victoria Archives*)

Was she Aileen? Photograph taken by Peter Stursberg. (*Courtesy Peter Stursberg*)

Victoria City Council, 1936. L to r. Back row: E. Williams, W. Luney, T.W.C. Hawkins, R.A.C Dewar, H.A. Wills, S.H. O'Kell. Front row: J.D. Hunter, J. Adams, D. Leeming (Mayor), P.R. Brown, A. McGavin. (*Courtesy City of Victoria Archives*)

Victoria Daily Times staff, 1934, on the grounds of the Empress Hotel. L. to r.: Lionel Backler, Peter Inglis, Peter Stursberg, Graham Harris, Pete Sallaway, Irving Strickland, Ted Fox, Nancy Hodges, Ken Drury, Bill Henderson, Roy "Cap" Thorsen, Bruce Hutchison, Jim Nesbitt, Les Fox, Archie Wills, Art Stott, Dick Freeman, Benny Nicholas, Harry Hodges, Mrs. H. A. Whillans, Cornelius "Mory" Moriarty, Frank Pagett, Tom Merriman. (*Courtesy Peter Stursberg*)

Peter Stursberg, working his way to Europe aboard a cattle boat, 1938. (*Courtesy Peter Stursberg*)

Peter Stursberg with two local girls at the ruins of Castle Durnstein, above the Danube River in Austria, 1938. (*Courtesy Peter Stursberg*)

24

In the leap year of 1936, there were so many "spinster" dances in Victoria, where the girls outnumbered the boys in any case, that most of these parties could not be held on February 29, although the best one was held on that date and, as might be expected, in the Empress Hotel. The Vancouver Island Publicity Bureau was said to be encouraging such a trend, as it wanted to promote Victoria as "the Leap Year town, where the women outnumber the men and take them to dances". Certainly this would have had more oomph than the "little bit of Olde England" stuff, and the "Follow the Birds to Victoria" slogan, but the bureau was just dreaming. There were never to be as many spinsters' dances again, not only because the next leap years were during the war, but because of what happened at these wild, wild parties. In fact the Jubilee Hospital Women's Auxiliary, which put on the Spinsters' Ball at the Empress Hotel, took a public pledge never to do it again.

Well, the roles were reversed, and we knew what it was like to sit around waiting for a telephone call, waiting for a bid to the dance. I recall that it was a tense, frustrating time, and that I began to sympathize with the lot of the female of the species, which is certainly inferior to that of the male. We were being paid back for our sins of commission, and I have to admit that the men in Victoria were spoiled, and never dated till the last minute; in fact, Lionel Backler considered it against his principles to make any social engagement in advance, and there was a friend of mine who would ring a girl up at 10 P.M. and expect her to go out with him that night, and often she did, which just showed how hard up the Victoria babes were. At any rate, Aileen let me stew for an unconscionably long time, or so it seemed, before inviting me to the Spinsters' Ball.

For the leap year festivity, the girls borrowed their father's cars, picked us up, provided camellias for our buttonholes, even took off our coats, and they did very well in their reverse roles, except for the drinks. Aileen had a huge forty-ounce crock of rye, which she made me carry into the hotel, and which was strictly against the spinsters' rules. I thought that she was providing the liquor for the whole party, as she was sharing a bedroom with four other girls (it was standard procedure at a big formal dance to have a room to drink in, since the main ballroom was cleared of all furniture except for a fringe of caned chairs), but then I saw a row of bottles of similar stupendous size on the bureau.

The trouble was that the girls had no experience in judging how much liquor should be brought to a party, and erred on the side of too much rather than too little — far too much: there was enough booze to start a brawl, and that is what it became: the Spinsters' Brawl. The oversized bottles of liquor on the bureau shocked "Four Eyes", the hotel dick, a man of medium height and nondescript appearance, neatly dressed in a dark suit, who wore a worldly smile on most occasions but not tonight; I saw him look into our room through the open door and shake his head as he turned and continued up the carpeted corridor; there was a similar display of potential trouble in every bedroom.

Downstairs, in the ballroom's vibrant roar, the music went round and round and so did the spotlights, and amid their changing colours, I recognized Brian Burdon-Murphy, who was a leader of the Beaux Arts set. The Burdon-Murphys had a flat opposite the *Times,* where they ran a school of dancing and elocution, and Aileen had taken me to an after-theatre party there which was very much on the theatrical up and up, but Brian, who had the blackest eyebrows you ever saw, was a good guy. One of Billy Tickle's trumpeters stepped up to the mike and recited more than sang: "Oh, I push the first valve down. The music goes down and around, whoa-ho-ho-ho-ho-ho, and it comes up here". The song had reached the pinnacle of its great popularity, and the swaying mass on the ballroom's creaking floor joined in: "The music goes 'round and around . . . and it comes out here". It was the white man's potlatch and the spinning spotlights provided the spirit masks. There was Jack Trace, looking like some forest monster, and my brother, silhouetted like a totem pole against the turbulent darkness of the rest of the ballroom.

Upstairs in the bedrooms, the conversation went 'round and around and became louder and louder as the levels in the forty-ounce bottles went down and down:

"Say, did you know that Robert Taylor's real name is Spangler Arlington Brugh?"

"You must be kidding — Spangler Arlington Brugh!"

"No, it's the truth, so help me."

"Well, who would have thunk it?"

"What's the matter with Spangler Arlington Brugh? I think it's more distinguished than Robert Taylor."

"Suppose that Jean Harlow was called Dotty Zilch. Wouldn't you like her just the same?"

"Dotty Zilch."

"Aimee Semple McPherson."

"Miss Fidditch, my ole school teacher."

"A rose by any other name would still be Jean Harlow."

It was two o'clock in the morning when Billy Tickle struck up "God Save the King"; the dance was over, but the party was beginning to reach a crescendo in the bedroom bars. Our room was as full and as frantic as a beehive; a fellow I didn't know was stretched out cold in the bathtub; a couple of babes were doing a soft shoe on one of the beds; a small group was standing with arms around each other singing, and above the reverberation of the conversation would come snatches of a favourite song of the times: "You ought to be in pictures". The quartet or quintet switched to "Who's afraid of the Big Bad Wolf", and their harmonizing interrupted a word game:

"Knock, knock."

"Who's afraid of the Big Bad Wolf, the Big Bad Wolf, the Big Bad Wolf?"

"Who's there?"

"The Big Bad Wolf, the Big Bad Wolf."

"Tarzan."

"Tarzan, who?"

"Tarzan Stripes."

The smashing of the glass top of the bureau was innocent enough; one of the self-appointed bartenders just banged a bottle down too hard, the clot, but the noise was such that nobody heard it, although it was soon apparent that something had happened. There were dire warnings about what Four Eyes would do. Some of the more inebriated took it as a signal to "break up the lousy joint", but they were restrained. An argument developed as to whether the broken glass top should be left on the bureau, or removed and the shards stacked in a cupboard, or thrown out the window. The moderates, or moderately drunk, prevailed, and there was no defenestration, although in the heat of the moment, one fellow did toss a pillow out the window. Then word was received that Four Eyes was coming down the hall, and there was a rush to get out, and despite the leap year, the girls neglected to help the boys on with their coats. Everyone was in too much of a hurry; it was each person (male or female) for him or herself.

We finished up at the Poodle Dog Café, spooning bowls of clam chowder and visiting other booths to exchange notes. Apparently, the brawl was worse elsewhere; the emergency fire fighting station on the second floor had been rifled and the hose dragged into one room and hung out the window, while the axes had been used to break down the doors of bathrooms and smash up furniture; several chairs and at least one bed were found in the flower beds surrounding the hotel. The next day in the *Victoria Daily Times*, the Jubilee Hospital Women's Auxiliary deplored the vandalism, announced that it would pay for the damage done, and took the pledge never to sponsor another Spinsters' Ball.

25

One of Ben Nicholas' extravagances was a two-toned (chocolate and dark gold) Graham Paige sedan, which he could not drive since he had never learned to drive — his assistant, Irving Strickland, the dour youth who occupied the sheep pen in the anteroom to his office, was drafted as chauffeur. The car was streamlined in the fashion of the times, and its headlights grew out of its fenders; the interior was soft and luxurious. Benny loved to take his boys, as the reporters were called, for a drive in this great drawing room of a car — and they were his boys. The editor's relationship with the younger members of the staff was more that of a father than of a boss.

At any rate, one spring day he persuaded Archie Wills to let me off early so that I could accompany him on a drive up-island to visit the Fairbridge Farm School, which had opened recently near Cowichan Lake; his excuse was that he wanted me to do a story on the school for the farm and garden page (still part of my editorial stint).

We set off after lunch, the editor rolling around like a great rubber ball in one corner of the back seat and myself in the other, holding grandly to a tasselled sash, with Irving up front behind the wheel, and drove out of the city past the Gorge, a narrow fjord where the pine-treed shore rose steeply from the sea. The water, sparkling and shimmering blue in the sunshine, and the rich greeness of the land, seemed to hold the promise of adventure, of travel to faraway places, just as the ships did, the masts and funnels that we saw from the *Times* windows, only they belonged to the ferry boats that went no farther than Seattle and Vancouver.

Yes, things were different now, Benny said as we bowled along in this jeezeling great car, there was a lot more education now. Why, he went on, in the old days, you had to learn on the job: that's what Archie Wills did, he came to the *Times* as an office boy, just a skinny kid but a bright little fellow, and besides hustling copy and writing obits, he swept up and did the jobs that the janitor now did. Some newspapermen began as printer's devils, helping in the shop, and that's how Harry Hodges got started. He had been a linotype operator before becoming an editorial writer, the editor said as he sucked on a corncob pipe, which dribbled bits of tobacco on the beige-coloured upholstery of the back seat.

Benny was a pipe sucker rather than a pipe smoker, just as he was a cigar chewer; when he wasn't doing either, he would rattle a peppermint around in his mouth, and he always had a bag of candy in his pocket. It was no wonder that he had the figure of a contented Buddha, for, as he himself claimed, sitting was his favourite sport; he did not believe in exercise — the human body was like a furnace, he said, "all you have to do is stoke it and leave it alone."

At the Goldstream, Irving slowed down on the insistence of the editor so that we could catch a glimpse of the salmon fighting their way upstream to the spawning grounds, leaping and hurling themselves forward in a fearful frenzy, as though being pursued by all the demons of the sea; it was an incredible sight, and the Goldstream, which had been named by some prospector for the colour he had panned, was flashing silver now as the great fish staged their annual struggle with the elements, made more dramatic by the broken light of the sun shining through the pine trees.

Jesus, what a sight, and I whistled and repeated an advertising slogan from radio: "Nature in the raw is seldom mild". The editor grunted and said it was the urge for reproduction or SEX, in upper case, that was driving these salmon crazy, so that they were bashing themselves to pieces in their attempt to reach the spawning grounds. He must bring some ministers, some of the mealy-mouthed men of God, who never allowed the word *sex* to cross their lips, and get them to explain this phenomenon, and Benny chuckled. He returned to talking about the changes in the newspaper business as we drove on.

In the old days, he said, the newspapermen were a rough and dissolute crowd, drunk disorderly, ill-mannered, and they used to spit on the news room floor. Ask Archie, Mr. Nicholas said, Archie had to sweep up, and as if he were thinking aloud, added that some of the reporters didn't seem to have any homes. There was one fellow who used to sneak back to the office late at night and stretch out on the telegraph desk, but the editor had to admit that this poor guy was escaping from a wife who must have been the harridan of harridans. There was a vagabondage about the old days, and he was talking about ten or twenty years ago. Newspapermen had become respectable now, Benny said, which was a good thing, but some of the fun had gone out of the business and he wriggled around to a more comfortable position in the soft divan at the back of the Graham-Paige.

We had reached the summit of the Malahat Drive and beneath us lay Brentwood Inlet, another fjord, and according to the tourist brochure on Vancouver Island, the most beautiful: the dark green forest, its surface broken by some ragged giants of Douglas fir, rolled splendidly down the steep slopes to the sea, which appeared to have the consistency of thick pea soup from this height; across the opaque waters were the scratches made by small fishing boats trolling for salmon. We could not see them, but we could be sure that the fishermen were lolling about, sunning themselves, or playing cards or drinking beer, while their rods were out over the stern, the lines strung taut as the boats chugged along so slowly they hardly seemed to be moving.

This was the lazy man's way of fishing, for the fish caught themselves, ringing a bell on the rods when they were properly hooked, rousing the somnolent fishermen from their dreams of piscatorial pleasures, from their poker or gin rummy games — they were lotus eaters all right. On the way down the other side of the Malahat summit, we drove past a panorama of snow-covered mountains, with Mount Baker's celestial eminence above them all, rising higher and higher as we slowly sank.

Great changes had occurred, Benny Nicholas repeated, and jabbed a pudgy finger in my direction (if we had been standing talking in the news room, he would have jabbed his finger into my ribs), and I was an example of these changes because I had been to university, as had Lionel Backler. We were the new kind of journalist, he went on, and I wriggled around on the feather-soft seat and felt warm with importance. Oh, there had been university men before on the editorial staff, and Ken Drury was one, but he was the exception, while we were going to be the regular run of reporters, fresh out of college, and Benny said that he didn't mean by that the Columbia School of Journalism — he snorted at the very thought of it, how could you be taught to be a newspaperman, it was preposterous, but he was in favour of the drive towards greater education for everyone.

However, there was a paradox involved: that with all the increased education, there should be this agitation for a union. Mr. Nicholas shook his head and grumbled as he reached into an inside pocket for his leather cigar case, selected a cigar and stuck it in the corner of his mouth; he would have thought that college boys would consider journalism a profession, instead of which they were degrading themselves and their work by joining forces with labour.

What utter bullshit, I thought, and wished that Lionel were with us, as I could never argue with the editor; I muttered something about wages being surely the cause of the discontent, and that fellows who had been to university expected to be paid more. I was getting $17.50 a week, and I knew that one of the linotype operators, who wasn't much older than I, was making more than twice as much as I was; he had shown me his weekly pay package which came to almost $40, for God's sake. What the hell, Benny was such a loveable old guy, such an understanding boss, but he had a nineteenth century approach to some things, especially trade unions. But then, I supposed that he was the representative of the capitalist classes, of the newspaper owners, who must be shaking in their shoes with the rise of the American Newspaper Guild — and the ANG was active just across the Strait of Juan de Fuca in Seattle.*

The visit to the Fairbridge Farm School was not a success; the new brick buildings stood naked, without a decorative shrub or flower bed, on rolling meadowland which was fringed by the dark shadow of the forest near Cowichan Lake. While Benny loved kids and was taken with the school plant, the barns and all the modern facilities for agricultural training, he found the snotty-nosed Cockney boys in their uniform of gray sweaters and black shorts rather reserved and withdrawn. Then, too, as he said on the way home, he wondered whether such British charities as the Fairbridge Farm School and Dr. Barnardo's Home should be allowed to operate in Canada and dump their unwanted children on us; it was treating the Dominion like a colony, but then the British still regarded us as colonials. Here was Benny railing against the imperialists as if he were Lionel Backler, and after that diatribe against the trade unions. There was a paradox, it seemed to me, but the editor was a man of many sides and many facets.

*A 1936 strike which closed the Seattle *Post Intelligencer* was the first significant victory of ANG over the Hearst chain.

26

As a result of the death of the sitting member, D. B. Plunkett, one of the Conservatives who had survived last year's Liberal sweep, Victoria was faced with a by-election in June of 1936, and it was common talk on street corners and in the city room of the *Times* that Benny Nicholas would be the Liberal candidate. After all, he had headed the local party association since God knows when and he had gone to Ottawa and served the Laurier government as executive assistant to the Honourable William Templeman. Politics was part of him, but he had never run for office.

When he was asked about the scuttlebutt, he would turn the question and inquire whether it was true because he hadn't heard anything about it, but his eyes would light up and a thin film of sweat would line his upper lip. Actually, during one of the bull sessions after the last edition had gone, Benny admitted that he was under considerable pressure to run, and that he might do so because there were things that he felt that he should do and say for Canada and Vancouver Island. But he added that if he did go to Ottawa, if he won the by-election, it would be the end of him in a couple of years.

No one doubted that he could win because he was so well known in the city and so well liked. It was said that King Gordon, who had run second for the CCF the last time, would not contest the riding against the editor, but this sort of speculation took the socialists for granted and in the light of hindsight, proved to be wrong. The fact that S.F. (for Simon Fraser) Tolmie, the former premier of the province, would be running for the Conservatives assured a contest, although we still thought it would be a runaway.

It was noticeable that the editor's speeches became more political that warm and balmy spring, and B. C. Nicholas was in great demand as a public speaker, not only in Victoria but further afield. He seldom turned down an engagement and his speeches were always enthusiastically received. One speech that he had made in Edinburgh at a meeting of the Empire Press Union was remembered and quoted for years: he spoke of Scotland and the sons of Scotland in Canada with such wit and wisdom that he enthralled the Scotsmen present and there were editorials of praise in the local press and the great national papers of Britain. This amused him somewhat, as he was the American-born son of a Cornishman.

I had to cover a number of his public appearances, and I marvelled at the way that he could hold an audience spellbound, even a convention audience in an advanced state of inebriation. This is the kind of thing he'd say, and the way he'd say it:

"You've heard politics described as the art of the possible," and Benny would pause for a moment, holding his audience in the toils of anticipation. "Well, the impossible is involved — because you've got to get elected to practice the art of the possible and in order to get elected, you've got to promise the impossible." (Laughter and applause might have been written into the script.)

"The politicians on the stump," he'd go on, "forget that if a man has a cow or a rosebush, he's far more interested in them than in all the affairs of state. And quite right, too. A cow or a rosebush is more important in the end than anything a government can do."

Democracy, according to the editor, reached its culmination in the town hall meeting of the old New England states; everyone participated, the well-to-do landowner and the humble tradesman, and there was no doubt that it was the most democratic assembly of all time. In the mass society of today, the vital question was whether democracy meant anything more than voting, the mechanical act of marking a piece of paper with your choice and putting that piece of paper in the ballot box.

"Your modern politician," Ben Nicholas continued, "is so concerned with establishing his identity that he spends most of his time going around from house to house, knocking on doors, and saying: 'How are you? I'm your candidate. I hope you'll support me.' He seldom discusses the issues and finds very few people willing to listen to him when he does hire a hall and speak. And so, electioneering comes down to saying: 'How are you?', and the way you say it, the sincerity in your voice, the quality of your smile, may make the difference between winning and losing."

Like most politicians, Benny had a master speech which he would update, as a good newspaperman should, but which was essentially the same speech; and I heard him tell the same jokes and anecdotes again and again; the editor would excuse this by saying that the public had a short memory, but there was also the fact that his stories were liked because of their familiarity.

Mr. Nicholas was concerned about the future of democracy. How could there be any participation, such as there was in the old town hall meetings, in a big city riding? There, the candidate's main task was to become known, and that was why a man who was already known had an unfair advantage over anyone else. When he said this, there was always a knowing hoot from the audience, and the editor would look surprised, and his great moon face, which was an actor's mask, would show bewilderment. He said he wasn't thinking of himself but of such celebrities as newspaper columnists like Bruce Hutchison and Jim Butterfield of the Vancouver *Province* and Bob Bouchette of the Vancouver *Sun* (he added the last two names because it was a province-wide audience he was addressing), and the radio announcers.

He would go on about the radio announcers — they got more fan mail than screen stars nowadays, and they should make very good members of Parliament because you could always understand what they were saying, even when they didn't have anything to say.

"I have no illusion about government," Benny would say, and standing there in his rumpled tux, resting his belly on the edge of the table, he looked like a bald and benevolent Friar Tuck. "It's a necessary evil. There is no government that's good, and some are very bad indeed. Governments make war — I don't see how they can escape the responsibility for that — and in the end, a government or governments will destroy the world. That's going to happen if we go on piling up armaments. It's our duty to try to restrain governments and let them do as little damage as possible, and to prevent them from committing suicide. And that, we know from experience, is a difficult and thankless task."

27

In the spring of 1936, as he had done in years before, Benny Nicholas went east to the annual meeting of the Canadian Press, of which he was a founder and long-time director; Archie Wills accompanied him. I wondered then why there was so much dread about this annual junket, and why the older members of the *Times* editorial staff, like Ken Drury and Nancy Hodges and even Archie Wills, would gossip in low tones among themselves and would appear to be embarrassed if the younger members of the staff, such as myself or Peter Inglis or the new, boyish-looking office boy, Bobby Drummond Hay, might have overheard.

At any rate, he went away, and there was the limbo that occurred whenever he was gone; we liked it because authority, even such a benevolent authority as his, had been removed, if only temporarily; and we didn't like it because we missed him. There was a lull in the news too because we were between the end of the Ethiopian War and the triumph of the Italian fascists and all things evil, and the beginning of the Spanish Civil War, which was to lead to the triumph of the fascists and all things evil. These were the doldrum days on the island of the lotus eaters.

When Benny returned, he looked very tired; there were dark smudges under his eyes, and his face, which had always been round and full, with the consistency of ripe cheese, was drawn, the skin hanging in gray folds. He didn't stop to say hello, which was unlike him, and stayed in his office without once putting his head into the news room.

On the fateful Tuesday, May 19, 1936 I could sense there was something wrong; people talked in hushed voices and I overheard someone say that the editor was a very sick man indeed; his assistant, Irving Strickland, looked darker and more dour than ever. It was after lunch when I was returning to my desk through the dark, partitioned hallway, where some soiled raincoats and battered fedoras hung, towards the newsroom, that I heard a scurrying in the editor's quarters. I went into the anteroom, and a distraught Irving Strickland rushed past me, gasping, "My God, he's dead". The door to the editor's office was open, and there, lying on the floor beside his upturned chair, was Benny; he was on his back, his knees bent, his face a glaucous colour.

Everyone and everything seemed in a daze, yet the paper came out on time, and the main story, headlined, B. C. NICHOLAS DIED SUDDENLY TODAY, and accompanied by an old round picture of the boss, was about his death:

Benjamin Charles Nicholas, editor of the *Victoria Daily Times*, passed away with tragic suddenness at 2 o'clock this afternoon after collapsing from a cardiac attack in his office chair.

Mr. Nicholas was unwell when he came to the office this morning but stayed at his desk. When he suddenly collapsed, Dr. Frank Bryant was immediately called, but medical treatment failed to rally him.

His tragic death will cast a shadow of mourning over the entire province as it did over the staff of the *Times* just at the hour when the paper was going to press. He was beloved of every man who worked under him.

The report was a full column long on the front page with a column long turn-over. It said that Benny was to have been the Liberal candidate in the Victoria by-election, and in fact, was to have been nominated at a party meeting that very night. Also on the front page that day was a report that King Gordon would be the CCF candidate again, a decision that must have been made some time before the editor's death. Much of the two thousand word main story on May 19, 1936 may have been a pre-prepared obituary, but considering the shock and emotion there was, only the old pros in the office could have written the lead and edited it.

28

Victoria and Vancouver Island had never known such an outpouring of grief for anyone as there was for Benny Nicholas. Not even the great Amor De Cosmos rated so many tributes. It was, as Rev. W. G. Wilson, the United Church minister, said when he conducted the obsequies in Hayward's B.C. Funeral Chapel, it was as if a monarch had died.

On the day after his sudden collapse and the dreadful frantic rush to get the story into print, the *Times* could do justice to its beloved boss. There was the latest picture of him on the front page, sitting like a Buddha in his office chair, his pudgy hands clasped before his ample stomach, a half-smile on his great round face as if he were listening to one of us, and the tributes began beneath his picture and filled the whole of pages 6 and 7. The editorial page was devoted to him, and the only editorial, which was a column long, was entitled OUR CHIEF PASSES and was signed with Harry Hodges's initials, *HCH*:

> Few knew the good he did without the slightest ostentation; but it may be safe to point out, perhaps, that in no direction was this more convincingly manifested than in his attitude towards youth. Nor is it inappropriate to say that it was because he retained to the last a lovable boyishness of outlook that the welfare of youth lay most dear to his heart. Only those privileged to know him intimately, and the recipients of his bounty, realize how many young men owe their start in life to his generous and timely interest. His benefactions were legion.

Beside the single editorial was a feature which filled the whole of the second editorial column, only it was in the smaller regular newspaper type; it was simply headed B.C.N., which was the way he used to initial copy, and the author, Ken Drury, wrote that Benny was so much a part of the *Victoria Daily Times* that the paper would never be the same without him, and more than that, Victoria would not be the same without him. Mr. Nicholas had made up his mind to run for Parliament, and he had talked so happily about his hopes and prospects only the day before his death:

> It is thus tragedy triple-distilled — tragedy for his own hopes, tragedy for those who were associated with him and his legion of

friends throughout the country, and tragical from the viewpoint of the greater service all looked forward to him rendering his community and his country.

The third column on the editorial page was occupied by the "Loose Ends" column, in which Bruce Hutchison said that the men who worked with Benny Nicholas would like to say something adequate about him, but it couldn't be done. Bruce reminisced about what a character the editor was, the sort of character that Dickens would have liked to write about.

He had the outside eccentricities which fix him forever in the memory — the careless, creased clothes, the shirt sleeves when he was working, the absurd woolly slippers he liked to wear in the office, his habit of getting you in a corner and jabbing his finger into your chest to drive home his points.

The rest of the page consisted of press reaction to his death, reprints of editorials in the Vancouver *Province,* the Vancouver *Sun,* and the *Vancouver News Herald*; the *Edmonton Bulletin* mourned his passing at the early age of fifty-seven and called him one of the most outstanding and best-known newspapermen in the country.

(Advertisements on the *Times* editorial page that day for Spencer's groceteria featured such cash and carry items as sirloin steak at nineteen cents a pound, rib roast at eleven cents a pound, and minced steak, two pounds for fifteen cents.)

Then, there was the message from the Right Honourable W. L. Mackenzie King, Prime Minister of Canada, and like its author, it was a bit formal and rather wily: the Prime Minister said he was doubly sad because he had heard that Benny had agreed to let his name stand for the Liberal nomination, as though he, Mr. King, hadn't phoned the editor three times and used the utmost pressure to get him to run. The message went on:

Mr. Nicholas has been one of my most valued friends ever since the days of the Laurier administration when he was here as private secretary to the Honourable William Templeman, Minister of Inland Revenue. He was one of our outstanding Canadian journalists, whose success was attributed to his unselfish devotion and the promotion of his country's highest interest.

From that, there was no telling how close their relations had been. They had both been bouncing young bachelors in Edwardian Ottawa, public servants on the move and probably had exchanged ideas and chewed the rag together because both of them were interested in what makes governments tick, and in the making and the moulding of the country. There was no doubt that Mr. King, who was a high mucky muck in the Department of Labour then called the editor "Benny" — everybody did — but did Mr. Nicholas call the prime minister-to-be "Willy" or "Rex", which was one of his nicknames? Benny didn't talk much about his days in Ottawa, so there was no knowing.

Strangely enough, Mr. King didn't make any reference to Benny's mother in his message, and yet there was one thing that the two bachelors had in common, and that was a saintly mother. However, Hon. T. D. Pattullo, Premier of British Columbia, expressed "sincerest sympathy" to his mother who survived him and "to whom he always showed most filial love and devotion". Duff Pattullo also spoke of the "peculiar gift" Benny had of grasping the essentials of a problem, be it a world problem or the humblest of personal problems.

On Friday, the day Benny was buried, Bruce Hutchison, writing in "Loose Ends", changed his mind:

> The other day it was said here that no one would write an adequate tribute to Benny Nicholas. I think now I was wrong. Out of the great mass of tributes in which everybody tried to say what was in him, one phrase seemed to me to stand out from all the others. It came from the pen of Dean Quainton, whom I know only by reports of his speeches and his occasional letters to the editor. The Dean said about Benny Nicholas: 'Who could feel mean in his presence?' That seemed to me to tell the whole story. It was all there. Nothing needed to be added or taken away.

29

Hayward's B.C. Funeral Chapel was on Broughton Street between the half-built Anglican cathedral and the downtown business section, amid a clutter of garages and service stations. The interior looked like a chapel, with oak pews and frosted glass windows; it was brighter than the dimly lit parlours which most undertakers seemed to think were proper for their gloomy trade. Around and about the plain altar were masses of flowers, not just vases of white lilies, but baskets of pink snapdragons and blue lupins and wreaths of red roses. The members of the *Times* editorial staff were pall bearers, and when we filed into the three rows towards the front that had been set aside for us, I noticed that the chapel was full, and many prominent people, including Premier Pattullo and Mayor David Leeming, were seated in heavy, mournful silence.

I didn't pay much attention to the bigshots because my eyes were caught by the sight of Benny on display. The coffin was open and was only a few feet from us, almost as close as when I sat opposite him, listening to him talk only short days before in his office. Only his worn and haggard appearance then, for he was ill, had gone, and so had the green pallor of death. His face was round and full again but his cheeks, which had always been the colour of old ivory, were now shining red with rouge; this was a powdered and painted Benny that none of us had ever known. "Jesus, isn't that awful," someone muttered in our pew. It was unnerving.

Poor Benny: in death, he had been dressed up in an immaculately clean tuxedo, when his clothes were always creased and food stained, and had been laid out in this silken-padded, super de luxe casket. Spread over the lower half, the part that was closed, was a floral blanket of pink roses, double white narcissi, blue irises, pink snapdragons, and in the centre, white carnations forming the numerals 30, the mark the newspaperman puts at the end of a story; this was from the members of the *Times* editorial staff.

Although the editor would have wanted to be buried simply and without any fuss, and the paper had said on the day of his death that it would be a small private funeral, his out-of-town relatives, who took over the arrangements from old Mrs. Nicholas, had other and grander ideas. They got Dr. Wilson to conduct the service and the presence of Lieutenant Governor Eric Hamber and most of the provincial government in the congregation encouraged him to deliver a fulsome eulogy lasting half an hour. In his grating Ontario accent, he spoke of "this great spirit who has passed" and of "this good and selfless soul"; he explained away the fact that Benny seldom went to church by saying that "our dear departed friend" had always told him that he regretted not being able to attend Sunday services more regularly "but this was due to journalism, which was such a hard taskmaster" and kept him away from God's house, although he felt that it did not keep him from God's work. I thought I heard a muffled snicker in the row ahead of us, quickly camouflaged by a cough. Most of us had heard the editor jeer at organized religion, although he was no atheist, nor even an agnostic, and would probably have called himself a Christian; he even preached on occasion in local churches, and had undoubtedly occupied Dr. Wilson's United Church pulpit more than once.

Meanwhile, there was Benny in his open coffin; he might have been listening to Dr. Wilson's glowing praise, only it didn't seem to be him any more; it was more like a wax figure than anything else. Still, his presence, however unreal it might be, at his own obsequies had a disturbing effect. The atmosphere in the crowded chapel seemed close and airless.

Now, Dr. Wilson, who was a spare man with a thatch of white hair, intoned the Twenty-Third Psalm: "The Lord is my shepherd; I shall not want." It was when he reached the fourth verse and spoke the sombre words "Yea, though I walk through the valley of the shadow of death, I will fear no evil: for thou art with me; thy rod and thy staff they comfort me", that one of the reporters broke down and started to sob. Godalmighty, a tough newspaperman bawling like this; I felt uncomfortable and stared at Benny, who lay unmoved on the cushions of his coffin, a bland expression of vacuity on his painted countenance. The reporter wept uncontrollably. I began to sweat but I felt easier and I knew that I wasn't going to do the same. Somehow his sobs had broken the tension.

Still, I was relieved when the funeral service finally ended, and we could walk slowly down the aisle with our eyes cast down, being careful not to jostle the bigshots who were engaged in the same mournful manoeuvre, out of Hayward's funeral home, into the clean, cool, refreshing air of the street.

30

Nobody is perfect, which is one lousy fact of life — or to put it in reverse and emphasise the positive, everyone is a sinner, which merely confirms what the church has been saying for God knows how many years, although I don't get this original sin stuff. And it is a good thing too that we do have our faults, our weaknesses, our failings, our vices, if you like to call them that, otherwise we would be a bunch of angels mooning around in the heavens. Nothing is black or white, everything is gray, but what's the matter with that? There's a good gray colour, the colour of the liberal with a small L.

What I'm getting at is that there are always two sides to a story, and I'm sure that Benny would want both sides of his story told. He would want his picture painted warts and all, even though it might be just a sketch and not a full portrait. It must be said that he was able to hide his vice or weakness from the younger members of the *Times* staff. I remember one time barging into his office with a galley proof or something — the door was open as it usually was, and I hadn't even knocked — and surprising him taking a swig from a pint bottle. He was startled and a cloud of annoyance crossed the map of his face; he put away the nickey in a bottom desk drawer and explained that this was medicine that his doctor had ordered. I believed him.

In "The Most Unforgettable Character I've Met" (*Reader's Digest,* September, 1949), Bruce Hutchison said that Benny always took "a tiny nip of brandy secretly" before preaching in the local churches and 'once when the bottle broke, ascended the pulpit in an innocent cloud of alcohol." This would seem to indicate that besides keeping a bottle in his desk, the editor carried around one on his hip, which was a common practice in those days and a hangover from the prohibition era. There was the fact that his dear old mother disapproved (of course, she knew), and that he did not drink in her presence, which led him to secret drinking and to keeping bottles hidden in desk drawers and in his bedroom.

To me in my innocence, Benny's death was due to overexcitement about running in the by-election — I took it for granted that he had a weak heart. It wasn't till later that I was told the whole story by Archie Wills, who accompanied him to the Canadian Press annual meeting in

Toronto on the fateful trip when the Liberal candidacy and his death were really decided. Here are the notes I made immediately after our conversation; they read like a diary, and the news editor did keep a diary, typing it out after the last deadline. I think they are the best way of presenting this postscript:

On the train travelling East were a number of Benny's cronies, includ ing the *Times* advertising manager, Bill Patterson, and the *Colonist'* publisher J.L., Jimmy, Tait. All were greatly interested in Victoria's championship basketball team, the Dominoes, who were playing Winni peg Maroons for the Western title.

During the stopover in Winnipeg, A.W. contacted the Dominoes and made them promise to wire train on the result of game which was being played that night. Stars of Victoria basketball were two sets of brother — Art and Chuck Chapman and Lynn and Muzz Patrick, later of hockey fame. Another leading player, Doug Peden, was brother of Bill "Torchy" Peden, who became a world champion six-day bike racer.

The wire was received at Chapleau, Ontario, saying Dominoes had won. This called for a celebration, and Benny began drinking.

He continued drinking in Toronto at Royal York Hotel where con vention was held. His friends kept sending up bottles of liquor which A.W. tried to hide. Not many hiding places in hotel room. Benny was drunk at annual banquet but didn't make a spectacle of himself, as everyone else drunk.

Next day, A.W. told Benny he had to sober up for dinner being given by Victor Sifton* at the Ontario Club. Benny took umbrage and said he could stop drinking whenever he liked. He made to throw glass into bathtub but banged his hand against wall, breaking glass and cutting vein. Blood spurted to the ceiling.

A.W. applied a tourniquet and rushed Benny to hospital where six stitches needed to sew up wound. On way out, he lurched against door and banged his hand and wound had to be restitched.

Still at hotel in Toronto. Benny was supposed to go to Ottawa to see Mackenzie King about the vacancy in Victoria. A Liberal hack, noted for losing elections, would be trying for the nomination. The editor couldn't go but had long and confused telephone conversations with the Prime Minister.

As a result, the bemused PM sent him a telegram asking him to name Liberal candidate. Ben said, "Archie, you're the man for the job." A.W. was an alderman in Victoria. (When he won, and he headed polls, the non-drinking, non-smoking news editor handed out ties to the boys in the newsroom!)

*Late publisher of the *Winnipeg Free Press*.

However, A.W. refused Benny's offer saying that the pay* wasn't enough to maintain two homes and the job too uncertain for a family man with three small children.

A week had passed and it was a lost week. Benny was still drinking in the hotel room; bottles were being sent up by Bill Patterson, Walter Thompson (CNR) and other advertising and publicity men, whose conference followed the editors' meeting.

Finally, A.W. announced that he had to get home to his family and had booked a drawing room on the next day's train. Somehow, he poured Benny aboard.

Just after leaving Toronto, the Victoria basketball team's special car was attached to the trans-continental train. The Dominoes had played the Dominion finals in Windsor and had lost.

A.W. had brought a couple of bottles of Scotch aboard but they were soon gone and he had to buy more liquor at Kenora.

Benny had reached the sordid state of alcoholism; he looked like a tramp, he was dirty, unshaven, and his clothes had been slept in. A.W. tried to keep him in drawing room for fear he would make a public disgrace of himself, but Benny insisted on entertaining the Dominoes to dinner in the dining car and drinking there, which was strictly against the law.

A.W. was getting little sleep. Once when he fell off to sleep, he felt hands around his throat; he awoke and switched on the lights to find Benny making a fumbling search for another bottle.

In desperation, A.W. hired a giant on the Dominoes named Red Martin as a bodyguard, paying him six dollars a day. Martin slept on the couch in the drawing room, A.W. on the upper bunk, and Benny on the lower bunk. Among the redhead's duties was restraining Benny from going around in his pyjama tops and persuading him to get dressed.

By the time they boarded the ferry boat in Vancouver, Benny had the DTs. He was shaking and looking ghastly; he was seeing things, snakes and so on, and feeling things, ants attacking his arms and legs. He was full of remorse. He knew he was drinking himself to death but he couldn't do anything about it, and he figured he was dying.

On their arrival in Victoria, Benny refused to go home. He was afraid of his little slip of a mother. So he stayed at A.W.'s house.

It was there, after he had dried out a little, that his decision was made to run. John Hart (provincial finance minister and later premier) and other Liberal bigwigs were contacted and they were delighted at the news.

*Four thousand dollars sessional indemnity for Parliament, with one session a year.

The next day, when he had cleaned up a bit, Benny went home. But he began drinking again from caches he had in the apartment.

A few days after his return, the editor was at his desk. Tuesday, May 19, 1936 was an important day, as Liberal nominating convention was to meet that night to name him candidate, and his picture was to be run on the front page.

Before going to an early lunch, A.W. asked Irving Strickland how the editor was; Strickland said he had complained of not feeling well.

On returning from lunch A.W. found a commotion in the outer office. Apparently, some of Benny's old cronies had visited him and while they were there he had had a stroke. A.W. entered the office and found Benny lying on the floor; he was dead. Strickland was distraught.

The coroner had to be called. This was before the last deadline, and A.W. told Ken Drury to take out the story on his candidature and replace it with his obituary.

For a few brief days, Benny was remembered and mourned, but the mist of time soon obscured him until it was difficult to picture him as he was — leaning forward in his editorial chair, his suit rumpled, the chewed-up stump of a cigar in his pudgy hand, his face alive with the story that he was telling — the sordid funerary image of the painted features got in the way. The memory of the editor faded but it would always be enshrined in the subconscious of those who had known and loved him.

31

There were visitors such as Richard L. Neuberger* that summer, and they helped to enlighten the gloom that was made more oppressive by the beginning of the Spanish Civil War. Of course, the main question as far as we were concerned was who was going to succeed Benny. The power struggle, if it could be called that, didn't last long: Ken Drury was named editor, and in retrospect, it was the only choice. Mr. Monteith, the tall, bony accountant, had more power and was acting publisher (a role that B. C. Nicholas combined with that of editor). There was a good deal of grumbling by Harry Hodges when he came up from his third floor office to the news room, but Archie Wills, who might have had a legitimate beef, kept quiet and seemed to be satisfied with his promotion to managing editor; he kept his desk in the news room and continued to be city editor and news editor as well.

Besides Dick Neuberger, who was from Portland, Oregon, and a leading newspaperman on the Pacific Coast, another visitor was Howard Costigan of Seattle; he came regularly to Victoria and spoke in the City Temple and the Shrine auditorium and other halls.

Howard Costigan was an impressive orator, and had a great presence on the stage, as he looked like the opera singer Lawrence Tibbets, only larger; he was the head of the Washington Commonwealth Federation, which was similiar to the CCF, only the WCF did not contest any elections but was a power behind the scenes in the Democratic Party of Washington State at the time. Howard was too well dressed and liked the fleshpots too much to be a real revolutionary, or even a socialist. Although he thought of himself as being in the tradition of the Wobblies, the Industrial Workers of the World, most of whose leaders (Big Bill Hayward and all) had fled to the Soviet Union, he was really an American liberal, if not more uncertain politically. Later he left the WCF to become a radio broadcaster on one of the Seattle stations.

Dick Neuberger was a kind of radical too, but everyone was a left-winger in those days. I was tremendously flattered to go out with him, a real, live *New York Times* correspondent, who had articles published in such great journals as *The Nation* and *The New Republic* and

*Late U.S. Senator from Oregon.

Harper's, and who had just written a book with another western news-paperman, Kelly Loe, on the Townsend Plan. He gave me a copy of his book which was called *An Army of the Aged,* and the date of his autograph was September, 1936. In his role as Pacific Northwest cor-respondent of the *New York Times,* Victoria was part of Dick's baili-wick; I recall that he came up more than once to look into plans the provincial government had for building a highway to Alaska.

I used to think of both Howard Costigan and Dick Neuberger as being much older than myself, but a few years make a lot of difference when one is young. Dick used to talk about his university days, when he was editor of the college paper and ran a satirical campaign against the fraternities. Every day there would be a box on the feature page saying that the Dekes or the Alpha Delts or some other Greek letter society had pledged a Duesenberg special or a Packard Straight Eight or a forty-foot Chris-Craft cruiser.

That summer of 1936 was another blazing hot summer and on July 10, the *Victoria Times* headlined the heat wave which, it said, was scorching most of the continent; the prairies were a dust bowl and there was no wheat. A few days later, there were the first news dis-patches of trouble in Spain, where a newly elected republican govern-ment was battling an uprising by rebels who had the support of the armed forces and various other conservative and right wing groups. New names appeared in the papers: Manuel Azaña, Emilio Mola, and the fat-arsed General Francisco Franco, the feudalist who became leader of the insurgents. First the rebels would claim gains, then the Loyalists, as the government forces were called. It was difficult to figure out what was happening. At the end of the month, a new word was emblazoned in the headlines — *non-intervention* — which sounded aboveboard but turned out to be a dirty word, to cover the dirty business of throttling the Spanish government.

We were scornful of the British and French leaders, the decadent Western diplomats, "the stripe-pants boys", who had worked out the non-intervention sellout. Costigan, who was a bit of a conspirator him-self and who believed in conspiracy, said that the Cliveden Set was behind it all, that Lord and Lady Astor and their ilk were the real rulers of Britain. Dick Neuberger tended to be a bit more cynical, as a great newspaperman should be. But everyone was agreed that it was dis-gusting all right, the sight of democracy strangling its own children. Here were the Italian fascists and the German Nazis fighting quite openly on the side of Franco and his Moors; the Condor legion was being formed by the brave Hitlerites to bomb the bejesus out of the Spanish women and children — and what were the goddam British and French doing?

Why, they had declared non-intervention and were preventing the government side from getting the weapons with which to defend themselves. (This was before the Russians entered the fray.)

However, we soon found that the Spanish Civil War was much more divisive than the Ethiopian War, where everyone seemed to be against the Italians, because the Roman Catholic Church was supporting Franco.

32

In December, 1936 the awful news that King Edward VIII was quitting his throne for the love of an American divorcee, Wallis Warfield Simpson, burst on a largely unsuspecting public in Victoria. Although the Seattle papers and other papers across the border had been carrying reports of the royal romance and the royal goings on for weeks and months, a self-imposed censorship prevailed throughout Britain and the Empire, including the independent Dominion of Canada, until a few days before the abdication. Those who had sworn at the "filthy, lying American press" (some of the papers containing the reports had reached the Island and had been read but not believed) and had even written letters to the editor condemning the "yellow journalism" in the United States, had to eat their words; they did so in horror and revulsion.

Old Bill Henderson fairly twitched with excitement. "Anaemic Jesus," he muttered as he headed up the wire copy, shaking the words out of his pencil, "the greatest revelation since the virgin birth."

While admitting that the abdication was a great story, perhaps the greatest story, most of us in the news room looked on the event as a complete anachronism, a feudal farce played against a background of dole and depression and of the sort of social revolt and civil war that was raging in Spain, but we were all astonished at the crowds that gathered outside the *Times* building to read the bulletins.

There they stood, the retired tea planters from Ceylon, the rubber estate managers from Borneo, the ex-Indian civil servants, the former Malayan and Hong Kong policemen, the old China hands, the one-time gunboat commanders who knew the road to Mandalay was up the Irrawaddy River, the missionaries and traders who had followed the flag from the Far East to Vancouver Island, the veterans of the imperial forces; they blocked Broad Street opposite the windows where the bulletins were hung and overflowed onto Fort Street. There they stood, in their hacking jackets and blazers and club ties, looking straight ahead, reading the awful news; some of them shook their heads and muttered that it was terrible, that it couldn't be worse.

It must have been Harry Hodges, and not Ken Drury, who wrote the main editorial on the abdication, as it spoke so well for those reading the bulletins, and Harry, who still had an English accent, would have a greater sympathy for them. The abdication, the *Times* editorial said, struck at the very roots of the British way of life: here was this Prince Charming who refused to do his duty — and all because of a woman. "It is not a pleasant thing to say," the editorial went on, "that the man who was Edward VIII has not measured up to expectations."

1937

33

The trouble with Victoria was that it was off the map, and as Aileen and others in the Beaux Arts complained, touring companies did not venture as far as Vancouver Island, at least not many did, and we were the last to get anything new. It was off the map of the mainland, all right. Yet, while this cultural isolation offended most of the younger generation, it delighted our elders. The fact that Victoria was off on one side from the chaos and the tumult of the world meant that they were left alone in sweet contentment to potter around the garden, to play golf, or to fish. In his book *The Unknown Country*, Bruce Hutchison analyzed this attitude:

> No one who has entered the Inner Harbor of Victoria, so far as the official records show, has ever wanted to leave again. It is the normal, accepted ambition of most Canadians to spend their last days here. This is the Island where Ulysses met the sirens. This is the land of the Lotus Eaters, and many of those original inhabitants are still here.

As this book was published in 1942, it could be said that the thirties, more than any other time in Victoria's history, were the days of the lotus eaters. Bruce Hutchison himself was one, and I am sure that he wouldn't mind my saying so. He was so much in love with the Island that he hated travelling and whenever he had to go abroad, did so grudgingly and was always glad when the trip was over and he could hurry back to Saanich and his home and garden. However, the effect that the inner harbour had on me was quite different to that which Bruce described, for the funnels and white masts of the ferry boats gave me itchy feet.

Everything was behind the times in Victoria, fashions, changes in styles, new movies, hit tunes, the latest fads, you name them and they took months to reach us. For instance, there was "Gloomy Sunday", the suicide song; it was just catching on at the beginning of 1937 and it was in keeping with the mood of the first winter of the Spanish Civil War. The Germans were pouring into Spanish Morocco, which Franco had turned over to them as a staging area, and the war was being talked about as a little world war; meanwhile the western democracies continued to strangle the Spanish Republic with non-interventions — and there was the *Victoria Times* headline FRENCH VOTE TO BAR VOLUNTEERS. The Moscow Trials had begun and by February, the first of the old bolsheviks had been shot. It was not a time for idealists. I felt depressed: everything was gray and gloomy. Gloomy Sunday.

By the time the chain letter craze reached Victoria, it had more or less petered out in the United States, although this was one depression phenomenon that didn't die but kept breaking out in odd places like a polio epidemic, in Kalamazoo or Moose Jaw or what have you, and there would be reports of Joe Zilch getting thousands of dimes or quarters or dollars through the mail. It never rained but it rained "pennies from heaven", as the song said. We heard these same reports when the chain letters started circulating in Victoria; they were always secondhand or thirdhand but they sounded reliable. It was never anyone you knew but somebody a friend knew very well. The first chain letters came from the mainland, from Vancouver and Seattle.

"Scratch out the first name on the list and send a quarter to that person. Make five copies and send to five people adding the name of the person to whom the letter is mailed below yours on the list."

This was a simple, multiple-of-five chain letter, but if the chain were not broken, it would produce 3,125 dollars or quarters or whatever, and there were chain letters which were multiples of ten!

"Why, if they had only started chain letters back at the time of the crash, there wouldn't have been no depression," one of the printers said, and he was only half-kidding.

It was bad luck to break the chain, and that was stated in the letters and often underlined, but this reliance on superstition didn't work and couldn't work. If it had worked, for pete's sake, people would have been spending all their time writing chain letters because they multiplied so rapidly and they would soon run out of money to send, even dimes. However, there were enough suckers in Victoria to keep them going for a month or more.

Everyone was taken in: I remember how excited Aileen was to get the first chain letter, how she waved it dramatically and announced that she would be off to England. At the height of the craze, a young fellow who was a sort of beachcomber opened a clearing house for chain letters in one of the brokerage offices (it may have been his father's) on Fort Street, but after a couple of days, the authorities closed it down as a gambling joint.

I have to admit that I subscribed to one of the chain letters. Although I said that I didn't expect to get any money, I was disappointed not to get a dollar or two. About the only person I knew who collected was the sports editor, Pete Sallaway; he had got in early and received twelve to fifteen dollars in the mail, or so he said, and I did see him open a couple of envelopes and take a dollar bill from each.

34

Nineteen thirty seven was a vintage year for politics, which could be a pretty zany business in Victoria: a provincial election was called for June 1, and it was to settle the unholy row that had split the CCF group in the British Columbia legislature — "unholy" because a clergyman, the Reverend Robert Connell, was the cause of the row.

Then, there was Oxford Group member Hugh Savage, who got himself elected on the four absolutes; absolute love, absolute honesty, absolute bull, and so on. (The Oxford Group was the forerunner of Moral Rearmament.) He made one notable speech in which he said that the people should put their trust in God and called for free beer; this delighted us newspapermen, since the Oxford Group in Victoria was very much opposed to liquor of any kind. But Hugh Savage, who was the editor and publisher of the *Cowichan Leader*, an up-island weekly, could get away with murder, as he wore hairy tweeds of a bilious yellow colour which were patched with leather and made him appear the very essence of an English country gentleman. Coincidentally, so did Nigel Morgan, the communist leader.

However, it was the split in the CCF ranks that concerned me most; it amused many but it distressed me, as I considered myself to be a socialist — and here was this dreadful public squabble. I cringed at the sneering editorials. What made me a socialist? Not the depression, but probably a book, written fifty years before, *Looking Backwards* by Edward Bellamy. There must have been a demand for it, as the Musson Company put out a hardback reprint at a price of sixty cents. At any rate, I joined a CCF club which met in the Metzger's farmhouse, in the dale past St. Michael's church. I never knew whether Dick Metzger, a thickset lad about my age, who organized the club, ever became a bigshot in the CCF. I attended a couple of meetings and then quit out of boredom.

So many people were calling themselves socialists that I wondered why the theorists figured that no party of that name could win in North America; they might have been right, but surely the Canadian party could have picked a better euphemism than Cooperative Commonwealth Federation. As I said, there were so many socialists, such a bewildering variety, from the Marxists who claimed to be non-Communist, to the non-Marxist, to the National Socialists who were Grade A fascists, and the Radical Socialists who were out-and-out capitalists. Even Clem Davies, the local radio priest, was calling himself a socialist, a Bible Socialist, and he was as much a reactionary as Father Coughlin. Some of the rural politicians were spouting nonsense about being agrarian socialists while holding high the torch of the family farm. A couple of tycoons in Vancouver, whom the New Deal would have labelled "economic royalists", had caught on to the new jargon to the extent that they were describing themselves as "industrial socialists". There were scientific socialists (the technocrats of Technocracy Inc.), and Christian socialists, and it was to the latter classification that Rev. Robert Connell belonged: they regarded themselves as the only true socialists and tended to be rather patronizing and "my-good-mannish" with the horny-handed workers. Even old Benny Nicholas spoke of himself as being half a socialist. He believed that eventually there would be a great deal of socialism in Canada, but it would not be called that, and he condemned the CCF for being in too much of a hurry.

Shortly after the CCF's founding conference in Regina in the summer of 1933, the British Columbia legislature was dissolved and an election called for the fall — the first real test for the new party. A provincial organization existed, but no provincial leader had been chosen. Ernie Winch was the obvious choice: not only was he a veteran socialist and prominent trade union leader in Vancouver, but he was a close confidant of J. S. Woodsworth, the saintly pioneer of socialism in Canada, who had been unanimously chosen national leader of the CCF at Regina. In fact, Ernie Winch was J.S.'s benefactor; he had provided the ex-minister with a haven after he had been driven from his Methodist church for preaching pacifism. Ernie also helped him to find a job as a longshoreman on the Vancouver waterfront. That was in 1918.

But Ernie was a bricklayer, hard and knobby, and his speech was in character. It was too crude for the clerics and professors, the soft-handed reformers who had flocked into the movement with the depression. They wanted Rev. Robert Connell to be the provincial party leader, and they got their way by insisting that the leader be chosen after the election by those CCFers who had been elected members of the Legislative Assembly. Although the Conservative government of Premier S. F. Tolmie was overturned by the 1933 vote, the provincial apple cart was not upset. The frightened middle classes switched to the other old-line party, and the Liberals were swept into power. Only seven CCFers were successful at the polls, including Connell, Ernie Winch and his son Harold,* but

*Since 1953, CCF–NDP MP for Vancouver East.

such was the Liberal landslide that this handful of socialist members became the official opposition.

Rev. Robert Connell, who was a most Christian looking gentleman with his neatly trimmed gray beard, never had any doubt that he should lead the CCF in British Columbia. His victory at the polls had given him a good deal of political glamour; it impressed the hell out of Ernie Winch. If this clergyman could carry Tory Victoria for the socialists, then perhaps he was the man to lead the party and bring to it the support of the god-fearing middle classes. So, Ernie concurred in his election as leader.

Although Mr. Connell had no previous experience in politics, he was supremely confident because as he said, "I know church politics and they're much the same." He was an Anglican minister and his accent showed that he had come from the old country, like many other members of the clergy on Vancouver Island.

From the beginning there was continuous turmoil in the CCF caucus. Connell had been too long used to the respect in which his cloth was held to argue with the Winches, especially the younger one, who kept glowering at him; yet, he had to deal with Harold as the caucus had named him whip. At twenty-six, the younger Winch was the youngest member of the legislature; he was dark and intense and looked like a gipsy, and a great political future was predicted for him, as he was a fiery speaker.

Beyond anything else, the clergyman couldn't abide the rough language old Ernie used. The church bazaar and union hall didn't mix. As a minister, the Reverend Mr. Connell expected to lead his flock, and he set out to do this, announcing policies which were not the result of consultation with the caucus but wholly his own idea. The Winches were goddam well furious. The Connell proposals cut across the tenets of the CCF. There was another row, and the reverend gentleman bore it as a Christian reformer should, without yielding an inch. To the clergyman, Marxists were anathema, they were atheists, Communists, anti-Christs; yet, the Winches called themselves Marxian socialists, although they claimed they were anti-Communist.

The final break came in 1936 when Rev. Connell, in his dog collar and all, stood up in the legislative chamber and denounced Marxists and Marxian socialists, and almost all brands of socialism. His speech was applauded noisily by the Liberal majority, and delighted Benny Nicholas who was still alive. In fact, the editor wanted to know why the CCF leader "had only now seen the light", and wondered whether Rev. Connell was speaking for all members of his party when he made this "clean breast".

He was not. That was soon made clear when a furious Harold Winch announced his resignation as whip the following day in the legislature. At the same time, he said that Connell had no right to continue to lead the official opposition since he had been elected as a member of the CCF and had deserted the party. However, the clergyman had decamped with three of his colleagues* and left the CCF a tripartite rump. It was an unusual situation. The speaker's ruling, which was really Premier Pattullo's, was that Connell, since the majority was with him, should continue as opposition leader. However, the new faction was given a separate caucus room.

Shortly after the break, Robert Connell formed his own party, the Social Reconstruction Party, and he and his three followers became members of this new group and were known as Social Reconstructionists, which was a bit easier to say than Cooperative Commonwealth Federation. However, the new party lasted not much more than a year, for all four were defeated in the 1937 provincial general election. All of which was explained quietly and with gentle humour by Colin Cameron,* who was more a social worker than a socialist, and used to visit the *Times* news room on behalf of the unemployed and those in relief camps up-island. According to Colin, the Reverend Mr. Connell might have known his church politics but he didn't know his congregation.

It was a just retribution for the Winches — the only other member who stood by them in the battle with the Connellites was Mrs. Dorothy Steeves. The CCF had seven members again in the BC House, and Colin Cameron was one of them, but the Winches were faced once more with the insistence of a professional man that the leadership should be his by right. This time, it was the smooth-talking Dr. Lyle Telford, the first radio doctor, who was famous because of his broadcasts, and who had been elected in place of one of Connell's followers in the Vancouver East constituency. For a year the legislative group had no leader, but finally the caucus brushed aside Dr. Telford's objections, and elected Harold Winch to the top job; old Ernie had counted himself out, saying that a younger man should be leader.

In the end, the domineering doctor followed the cleric out of the party. He got himself elected mayor of Vancouver, and the provincial CCF party saw this as an opportunity to get rid of him by adopting a ruling that a member could hold only one elected job. According to Harold Winch, Dr. Telford wasn't given a chance to resign but was expelled.

To top off the political year 1937, there was another federal by-elec-

---

*These were Jack Prince, Vancouver East; Ernie Bakewell, Mackenzie; Robert Blachford Swailes, Delta.

*Late CCF–NDP MP for Nanaimo–Cowichan–the Islands.

tion in Victoria; this was caused by the death of Hon. S. F. Tolmie, the former premier of the province, who had won the fateful by-election the preceding year when Benny Nicholas was to have been Liberal candidate. Pinkie McKelvie was nominated Conservative candidate and played down his ideas about an independent Vancouver Island during the campaign; the fact that he was running for office was the pretext given by the *Colonist* for demanding his resignation, although he left the paper on the first of May and the by-election wasn't held till late November. Once again, for the third time in three years, King Gordon returned to Victoria to run for the CCF, but though he increased his vote, he came last this time. R. W. Mayhew, the Liberal, won with a comfortable majority over McKelvie.

35

About the time we heard that Lionel Backler had gone to Spain to join the International Brigades, I became involved in an attempt to organize a Victoria chapter of the Veterans of Future Wars. How we got the news about Lionel, I never found out; Ken Drury, the editor of the *Times*, seemed to be the source of the information, and he was probably told by the local Spanish War Committee, which was an off-shoot of the Communist Party. At any rate, Bill Henderson said that Lionel was a damned fool, that he was too tall to dodge the bullets, and most of us gloomily agreed. There was an ominous sense of doom and disaster in the news room that day.

As for the Veterans of Future Wars, it was the latest rage in the United States, and the papers had pictures of college students parading with placards announcing that "future veterans demand immediate payment of bonuses", and "we want homes for future orphans now". It seems to me that George Cameron had something to do with organizing a local chapter, but I might be wrong. It was certainly the sort of gambit that would have appealed to him, for he was a sardonic guy, and you could never tell from the slow drawl that he affected (he had been born and educated in the United States) whether he was being sincere or satirical.

George lived in a large wooden house in Rockland, as his father was a lumber baron and there were Cameron mills in Victoria and up-island. He had a suite in a wing of the house, with bedroom, bathroom, and a study that was carpeted from wall to wall and lined with books. He also drove a late model car. Come to think of it, I had another new old car: before it broke up, I had turned in the Essex on a Rockne, the car that Studebaker named after the late Knut Rockne, the American football coach; it was a sports coupe and a very snazzy job too, with free wheeling and synchromesh gears, as well as a rumble seat.

The Veterans of Future Wars started as a lark at some American college (several claimed to have had the idea first)* and immediately caught on and spread like a forest fire throughout the continent. It represented the mood of the times, a hopeless, cynical mood that was the

---

*Columbia University of New York probably had the best claim.

result of all the wars there were, the Japanese invasion of China, the Ethiopian War, and now the Spanish Civil War, and the way that nobody dared to stand up to the fascist warmongers — we were drifting inexorably to another world war, and we should all be war veterans. There grew up a whole lore based on the past future tense: Mothers should receive gold stars for the sons that they will have given their country; pensions and bonuses should be paid immediately to future veterans. Coeds formed women's auxiliaries: the Widows of Future Wars.

Some old soldiers might have objected, and certainly the Veterans of Foreign Wars did, but the Veterans of Future Wars was mild stuff compared with a satirical article I read which likened the American gold star mothers to particularly productive beef cows. But what would a local chapter do if it were formed? There was no one to demonstrate against in that neck of the woods, no German or Italian consulates in Victoria, not even a British or French one. They might have paraded outside one of the Canadian Legion clubs but they would only be disturbing a bunch of beery old sweats, who wouldn't know what the hell was going on in any case. The proponents of the Veterans of Future Wars realized this and nodded their heads sadly. Victoria was really the end, the end of the world, the arsehole of creation.

But they wouldn't give up without a struggle. How about sending a cable to that mealy-mouthed son of a bitch, Mackenzie King, and telling him what a shit we think he is? Satisfying as that could be, it was hardly a reason for forming a dues-paying organization. Finally, the suggestion that a blow should be struck for pacifism by having toilet paper printed with Union Jacks was greeted with cries of derision. Kid stuff. And so it was, and that was the end of the attempt to set up a Victoria chapter of the Veterans of Future Wars.

36

Like most newspapermen whose work is writing, Lionel was a lousy correspondent, and in the eighteen months that he had been away, I got only a couple of letters from him, one of them a pencilled note from Spain. He did not even write to his parents very often, although he was very fond of them both, especially his mother. However, his last few letters have been kept by Bill Jack of Hatzic, B.C. among his own papers; Bill knew Lionel when they were students together at the University of British Columbia and in fact, shared a room with him in the fraternity house where they were living. From these letters and conversations with Hugh Garner, who fought in Spain with the XV Brigade, I have tried to reconstruct how Lionel came to join the International Brigades and his arrival at the front.

In a letter to his mother and father, dated simply "Sunday, June 27, Spain", Lionel told his parents that he had "enlisted to fight fascism" and asked for their understanding and that they be "proud of us". He wrote in pencil on a perforated sheet of paper which was torn out of a notebook:

> Everywhere here the people hail us — they hate Hitler and Mussolini as we do. I think, Mother, you'll understand immediately that something like this was inevitable for me. It was what I have felt for so long. Some of my best friends are here — and more are coming. You may have read about the International Battalions (sic). We are in good hands.

At the beginning of his letter, which was not long, Lionel said that he couldn't tell them how he got to Spain, and following this sentence, there were four lines heavily pencilled out, which might have been the work of the military censors.

Most Canadians sailed from New York for Spain, and Lionel would have certainly done so, as he was living there at the time he decided to stand up to the "fascist murderers". It wasn't difficult to join the International Brigades anywhere in Canada, as the Communists had agents in key places, but most of the drafts were made up in New York. Before embarkation, the volunteers were outfitted at an army surplus store on lower Broadway with an old U.S. uniform, great coat, boots, socks, shirt, underwear, all 1917 stuff but quite serviceable and packed in a black suitcase. There was not much secrecy about the movement of the men (despite the military censorship in Spain), and they were easily identifiable since each one of them carried an army surplus black suitcase as he boarded ship — they travelled third class — but the American officials paid no attention and asked no questions.

From the time the first draft left New York in December, 1936 every ship crossing the Atlantic carried recruits for the International Brigades, and a big liner like the *Berengaria* would have more than a hundred aboard. The volunteers were of all political stripes, socialists, liberals, Democrats and Republicans, but most of the Americans were Communists, and the leadership was Communist. Each draft of a dozen or so men usually had a party member at its head.

Paris was the main staging area for the Spanish Civil War, and the volunteers were billetted around the Place de Combat,* if you please, which was a tribute to the French sense of the fitness of things. They were officially enlisted in the International Brigades by a representative of the Spanish government. Then, when enough had assembled, they left in a special train. This was the most thrilling part of the journey: there had been no time for disillusionment, and there was wild enthusiasm among the 500 or so volunteers on the train, who shouted greetings and slogans and sang revolutionary songs in a dozen different languages.

In the early days the French authorities cooperated in the movement of volunteers. However, by the time that Lionel Backler arrived, the policy of non-intervention was being strictly applied, and the men had to dodge French police and border patrols. The crossing into Spain became a nightmare that haunted many of them long after the war was over. In small groups, they climbed the Pyrenees on foot, following guides who were probably smugglers; they were not allowed to smoke or talk for fear of giving the route away, and in the darkness they stumbled blindly over rocks and icy streams, to arrive almost dead from exhaustion at the Spanish border.

When they did, they let out a cheer, with practically their last gasp, but there was no response from the Spanish border guards, who just stared at them. This was the first shock — not all the Spanish Loyalists liked them. The border guards were Trotzkyists or members of the anarchist brigades, and much of Catalonia was anarchist in sympathy. The first night was spent in a castle, a great stone fortress which served as a transit camp for the Spanish Republican Army. The men bedded down in a cavernous hall that had been turned into a general dormitory, and the Canadian and American volunteers, whose moral outlook was reactionary although their politics might have been progressive, were amazed to see Russian women, Red Army doctors and nurses, sleeping in the same room as men.

*Renamed Place Colonel Fabien after a 1944 resistance hero.

Another troop train took them along the Mediterranean coast, and after Barcelona, the international volunteers got a warm welcome; they were cheered at every station and were given baskets of fruit by the peasants, who refused any payment. Their destination was Albacete, which was inland from Valencia and was the depot town for the International Brigades. The day after their arrival, the volunteers were paraded in the local bull ring, addressed by political commissars, and asked what units they wanted to join.

When Lionel reached Albacete in the late spring of 1937, the Canadian battalion, which was to be known as the Mackenzie-Papineau battalion, was being formed. Probably he got more than the cursory two week training course given most of the volunteers, which consisted mainly of infantry drill and learning how to operate a Russian Maxim machine gun because the "Mac-Paps", as the Canadians were called, were much better trained that most of the foreign units and became the shock troops of the XV International Brigade. At that time, the XV Brigade included the main American battalion, the Abraham Lincoln battalion; the Dimitrov battalion, made up of Central European refugees from fascism; the mixed French-Belgian battalion, known as the Franco-Belge battalion; and the British battalion. About a dozen languages were spoken in the Dimitrov battalion, and in order to reduce the babel and simplify the orders of command, it was decided that the XV Brigade should be English speaking, except for the Spanish battalions attached to it. So the Dimitrov and Franco-Belge battalions were transferred to other brigades, and the newly formed Mackenzie-Papineau battalion added — but that was not till the fall of 1937.

The Abraham Lincoln battalion was really the mother unit of the Mac-Paps, and it is possible that Lionel Backler, in the course of his training, was posted to temporary duty with the American battalion while it was still entrenched on the Jarama Front; the main battle was over and there was not much beyond patrol activity and the odd "poop-offs", when there was a lot of firing at nothing. Hugh Garner was with the Lincolns on the Jarama Front and he recalls that just behind their lines was a great mansion, surrounded by formal gardens, which served as brigade headquarters. The place had been ransacked, and about the only things left were autographed photographs of bullfighters hanging on the panelled walls. The Spanish grandee or whoever it was who owned the house must have been a bird fancier, as there were large bird cages in the garden; the feathered prisoners had been released with the revolution but — would you believe it — they had been replaced by human prisoners. The brigade used the cages as lockups for drunks and others on detention.

37

My job on the *Victoria Daily Times* was beginning to pall: after the early morning turn on the telegraph desk, and Bill Henderson seemed to be more crotchety than caustic in his comments, there was the dreary round of the hotels, unless Archie Wills had a special assignment. I was still doing the farm and garden page: in fact, I could see that I would never get rid of this chore until I left the paper. The sea looked bluer and more inviting than ever, and the sight of the ferry boats in the inner harbour, and of the ocean liners which all too infrequently docked at Rithet's pier, made me think of Spain, and of Lionel Backler and the International Brigades fighting on the dry hot hills under the bright hot sun, and of all the famous writers and foreign correspondents who were there, like Hemingway and Dos Passos and Malraux and Pierre van Passen.

Actually, the news from Spain was confusing: one day, the Loyalists seemed to be winning, the next day, the rebels. It depended on which reports the telegraph editor played up, and Bill had become very cynical about the Spanish war news. "Let's give those fascist buggers the headline this time," he would say as he sliced up the teletype copy with his steel ruler. One thing certain was that Bilbao had fallen.

Lionel's letter was not much help because he wrote about a "great offensive" but he didn't say where the fighting had been; perhaps the censorship wouldn't let him. He must have been referring to the attack on Brunete, west of Madrid, which was the first major government offensive. However, there is no mention of this place in the *Times* file of that period; there were dispatches datelined Madrid, which spoke of government advances and of the Loyalist threat to the fascists in the University City.

In his letter, Lionel said that he had been playing ping pong behind the front or at Albacete (apparently, some benefactor had given the Abraham Lincoln battalion several ping pong tables), and that this reminded him of our games at the Coach Lines depot in Victoria. There was a recreation room at the depot which was only a block down Broad Street from the *Times*, and we used to play there with the bus drivers and the dispatchers. Lionel was a pretty good player with a long reach which matched his six foot seven inch height; I played on the Coach Lines team in the city table tennis league but I don't know whether he did or had left by then.

There was not much else about himself in the letter; most of it dealt with the conduct of the civil war and Spanish politics. He said that the fall of Málaga was the result of the awful incompetence of the government. He seemed to have lost his enthusiasm for the republicans, but then it was apparent that this was the view of the communist militants in the International Brigades, as he kept quoting the political commisar (probably, the battalion's commissar) throughout. The fact that Bilbao had been taken by an Italian expeditionary force was due to disunity and even treachery among the Basques. And the political commissar made it clear that the so-called socialists in the government headed by labour leader Largo Caballero were to blame and even hinted that some of them might be fascists. As for Cabellero himself, he was just a big bag of wind. Fortunately, he had now been succeeded by Dr. Juan Negrin, and as a result of stronger and more resolute leadership the offensive had been launched.

Perhaps because of the censorship, Lionel didn't say much about the fighting, except to note that the Moors who were helping Franco win back Spain for Christendom always used the church belfries as snipers' nests — and these were the bastards who accused the republicans of defiling the churches. Altogether, some seventy thousand Loyalist troops took part in the Brunete offensive, and their objective was to cut the fascist lines of communication with the University City and thus relieve Madrid. For the battle, the brigade was divided into two regiments, one consisting of the Abe Lincoln and Washington battalions, and the British battalion, and the other of the Dimitrov, Franco-Belge and Spanish battalions. The republican forces took Brunete but had to give it up as a result of a counter-attack in which the enemy used his considerable air force to full advantage.

In his letter, Lionel complained about the way they were being bombed, even when they were in reserve. There was a big Italian Savoia bomber which came over every now and then and scored near misses in the fields beside the camp. Most of the fascist planes, however, were German Heinkels and Junkers, with the Luftwaffe iron cross and swastika markings on their wings. The Loyalists had hardly any planes compared with the hundreds that Hitler and Mussolini had supplied the rebels, and that was the trouble, Lionel said, because while the republican forces had shown that they could take to the offensive, they were not going to win the war without planes and more planes.

128

38

It was a dull September day, with the clouds hanging low over the city and menacing the ships at the end of Fort Street, when we got the news that Lionel Backler had been killed. I was in the news room telephone both, whose sides were covered with all sorts of strange hieroglyphics, odd numbers and queer doodlings that looked as though they might be masks for pornographic pictures, when I overheard someone say, "My God, poor Lionel's dead." Once again the information had come from the local Spanish Committee, which had received a wire from the headquarters of the International Brigades. The day was so dark the lights were on. I felt quite sick and put the receiver on its hook in the middle of a call.

There was a murmur of sorrow in the news room. Bill Henderson swore and repeated what he had said before, that Lionel was a damn fool to go to Spain because he was too tall to dodge the bullets. I didn't feel like talking. About all the news that Archie Wills had was that Lionel had fallen in action on the Aragon front, and that he had been cited for bravery and buried with full military honours at Murcia.

A whispered wake had begun, and I wanted to get away from the gloom in the news room, and the naked light bulbs shining in the daytime. Somehow, I found myself walking along Fort Street toward the inner harbour. The overcast made the light yellowish-gray, and the street looked mean and nasty, as did Government Street and View Street and Broad Street; I had never realized what a depressing place Victoria was until then.

I thought of Lionel's parents. I didn't really know them. I had met his mother once when I had called around to pick up Lionel to go on a pub crawl or some such excursion. He lived in a fine house in Oak Bay, which was surrounded by a high hedge.

His father, a retired British naval officer and a pretty high one at that, must have found his son's radical convictions incomprehensible if not embarrassing — he probably never talked about them when he visited a wardroom at the Esquimalt naval base or had lunch with cronies at the Union Club. Yet according to Bill Jack, the old man was proud of his son going to Spain and joining the International Brigades to fight for what he believed in.

The last letter that Lionel wrote was addressed to his mother and has no date. It was written as before on a sheet of paper torn from a notebook:

P.S.   Return Address
Please write   SR1 271
by return   Plaza del Altozano
                                      Albacete, Spain.

Dear Mother:

I know I am causing you suffering. I wish it could be otherwise. Let me tell you: I am happy. I am in splendid health — brown and hard under the Spanish sun. Truly, you will say: But I worry for his safety. Yes — But I feel everything will be all right, and that when I see you in about a year on my way back (and I mean to get out West) you will be proud of my appearance, my health and spirit, and of what I have done.

Here I am two months in Spain and going strong. I wish you could see our Canadian-American Battalion (the Mackenzie-Papineau). There are 25 or more from Vancouver. Our leader was formerly an instructor at the University of California, I believe. We have writers, painters, working people of all sorts, a father and son. The very best are here resolved to put an end to the monstrosity of organized murder.

Our assistant company leader is a German — and when I look at him I sometimes think how Dad would approve his bearing and appearance.

I am now a sergeant and third in command of a section of 36 at full strength. I have 12 men under my full command, subject to the higher officers.

We sergeants get pay which we hardly know how to spend. We have learned a great deal of military science — and often I march proudly at the head of my section when the other two leaders are not present.

A. E. Smith of Canada (a former parson) spoke to us a few days ago. He will tour Canada speaking for us — and mother dear I want you to hear him and I want you to join the Friends of the Mackenzie-Papineau Battalion. (Mackenzie was the grandfather of the present Canadian Premier — and nothing like him.)

Please get behind all the boys who are like your son. We have a job to do — a tough one — but we are going to do it along with all our friends in the world.

I have seen things here and learned things which make a man inches taller, so to speak. I want you to read Gorki's *Mother*, which I once mentioned. Please get it. It will make you understand.

Good night, mother and dad.
L.

Although there was no date on this letter, it must have been written at the same time as another letter to "Dear Comrade", dated August 17, 1937; the latter, which was addressed to the Students' League and printed in the *Ubyssey* of January 18, 1938 was found among his effects. If that was the right date, then he wrote the letter to his mother one week before he died.

Lionel Backler was mortally wounded on August 23, 1937 during the Loyalist capture of Quito, one of the fortified towns before the rebel stronghold of Saragossa, and died the following day; he was buried at Murcia. The Mackenzie-Papineau battalion did not enter the fighting on the Aragon front until October 13 when it bore the brunt of the attack on Fuentes de Ebro, another of the fortified positions before Saragossa. In his book, *Britons in Spain*, William Rust says that in this engagement, the Mac-Paps experienced "their baptism of fire, advanced nearly eight hundred yards and dug in on a ridge facing the enemy positions on the outskirts of town".

Yet, in his letter, Lionel wrote about being a sergeant in the Mackenzie-Papineau battalion. The explanation may be that, in order to gain experience, some of the Mac-Paps fought with the Abe Lincoln battalion at Quito, or that the Canadian unit was an outgrowth of the American battalion and was still part of the latter at the beginning of the advance on the Aragon front.*

---

*In *The Mackenzie-Papineau Battalion*, Victor Hoar says that "replacement drafts" were taken from the Mac-Pap ranks and sent to the Aragon front. He does not include Lionel Backler among Canadians he lists as killed or missing in Spain but acknowledges that his list is incomplete.

39

Aileen had left, as so many young people had, and I had no steady girl friend, which was the wrong way of putting it because I didn't believe in going steady with anyone. Her departure left me without any great sex interest, and very little interest of any kind. There was nothing for young people to do in Victoria, or not much. The lotus eaters liked it that way, and you couldn't blame them for not wanting any more sawmills spoiling the outskirts of the city or machine works cluttering Esquimalt harbour.

At any rate, Aileen had got a job singing in some flyblown night club in Vancouver. She had wanted to be an actress, but there was nothing but the Beaux Arts and amateur dramatics and there was always the danger of falling victim to the sort of itinerant director who preyed on would-be thespians in small towns, those with "star dust in their eyes". Major Bullock-Webster had a theory that the way you could tell a director was a phony was when he wanted to stage his own play. This happened more than once in Victoria, and Aileen took part in a performance at the Empire Theatre which was a real stinkeroo. Whew, was it ever!

Vancouver was in a state of turmoil then, however, from what she said in her letters, Aileen never noticed it. The relief camps had been shut down, but though times were better, they were only slightly better. There was still not enough work, so that with the first chill of fall, the single unemployed stopped riding the rods and made their way to the Pacific Coast, where there would be less danger of freezing to death. As might be expected, the civic authorities didn't relish having them in Vancouver — in fact, these worthies would have preferred the jobless to freeze to death, so long as they didn't know about it.

Towards the end of 1937, they cracked down on tin-canning on downtown Vancouver street corners, which was the unemployed's chief means of support. If anything, the unemployed were more highly organized now than they had been two years before at the time of the abortive march on Ottawa. They had a new leader, "Steve" Brodie, who was not as sinister a figure as Arthur Evans and who claimed not to be a Communist, although the Communists supported him. When the police arrested one tin canner, they found that they had arrested hundreds, and there was bedlam in the courts as the prisoners shouted slogans and sang songs. One of their favourites was an old Salvationist hymn, "Oh My Comrades, See the Signal". The chorus ran:

> Hold the fort, for I am coming;
> Jesus signals still;
> Wave the answer back to heaven:
> By Thy grace we will.

This they bawled out with great vigour, to the obvious embarrassment of the magistrates, who didn't know how to stop the "Commies" from singing hymns. There were so many of them convicted that the old relief camps had to be reopened as temporary prisons.

Next came the sit-down strikes. Having been driven off the streets by the city ordinances barring tin-canning or tag days, the unemployed occupied the main post office and other public buildings. Finally, Prime Minister Mackenzie King ordered the Mounties, "Mackenzie King's Cossacks", as they were now called, to evict them from federal property, which they did after a bloody riot. Then, Steve Brodie and the other organizers decided to march on Victoria, and the Vancouver city fathers were so delighted to see them go that they paid their way to the Island.

40

In December, 1937 our hopes were raised by the great Spanish republican victory at Teruel. About the same time, Dr. Norman Bethune visited Victoria. He was the famous Montreal surgeon who had developed the mobile blood transfusion units which were to save so many lives in Spain, and he was on a cross-country speaking tour to raise money for them. It was shortly after this that Dr. Bethune left for China, where he died a year and a half later while serving with the Communist guerilla forces; he was to become the greatest hero of the Chinese people and the Canadian who is known to more people in the world than any other Canadian.

I had to interview him and the only place I could see him was in the drug store next to the *Times* Building, where we had morning coffee. There were others who wanted to talk to him and were standing around him at the counter and he seemed preoccupied and even withdrawn; at times, he would say nothing and just stare into his coffee cup. When I asked him if he had seen Lionel Backler, he said that he had met so many that he couldn't remember and when I pointed out that Lionel was difficult to forget, as he was more than six and a half feet tall, he looked at me with his bright blue eyes and through me at the other people and through them. Despite his moodiness, Dr. Bethune gave the impression of serene confidence; he had on a dark sweater, with the red and white flash and gold star of the Spanish Republic worn like a decoration on his breast.

A large crowd turned out to hear him that night, and you could feel the waves of tension in the jam-packed hall that broke into roars of applause. A lonely figure in what seemed to be the uniform of a Spanish partisan, caught in the dusty golden beams of the spotlight, Dr. Bethune spoke of the attempt to portray the fascist invasion as a crusade to save Spain from communism, and called this not only a lie but "a calculated and vicious insanity" — and there was that roar from the crowd. "History will take revenge on those who have failed Spain," he said — and again that gunfire applause.

There was an arrogance about Dr. Bethune that Lionel shared, the arrogance of certainty; he had no doubts, he knew what was what and why, he had all the answers.

In December of 1937, during a Christmas offensive on the Aragon front, the Spanish Loyalists had seized the strategic town of Teruel — and there was that unforgettable picture of Hemingway manhandling a gun into position during the battle — the picture of an author as his own hero. It was the high-water mark of Spanish republican fortunes; after that, there was no place to go but down. By the middle of February, 1938 the fascist rebels retook Teruel.

1938-1939

41

Around the bolts in the ceiling were lumps of white paint, and they attracted my attention as I lay in my single berth cabin on the night boat to Vancouver, feeling twinges of home sickness; I could pick out those blobs of paint and tidy the ceiling if I had one of those boy scout knives with a thing to lift stones out of horses' hooves, ha ha, but I felt sad.

I had made the break and was leaving Victoria. My father had given me an advance of five hundred dollars, which allowed me to go overseas, and Ken Drury said that he would try to get me a job on Fleet Street through the Empire Press Union. This was an exchange arrangement, he explained, whereby an Englishman could come to Canada and work as a reporter while a Canadian could go to an English paper, but it didn't work very well. However, he would write to Henry Turner, the secretary of the Union. Meanwhile, I had six months' leave of absence from the *Victoria Daily Times,* but Archie Wills when he said good-bye, shaking my hand with that firm YMCA grip of his, said that I wouldn't be coming back, that young fellows when they left never came back.

I switched off the light. The ferry boat creaked and sighed, and the pipes above my head made a soft moaning sound. I thought of home and my mother's cooking, of the fire burning in the living room grate, of the sweet scent of pines at our place, of Jack Trace and George Cameron and my other friends, of Gilroy and my brother working in the woods, of Aileen and all the Aileens I had known, which reminded me of my last car, the smart Rockne coupe that I had sold to finance this trip, of Les Fox and Jimmy Nesbitt and Peter Inglis and the fellows on the *Times,* the familiar clutter of the news room, knee-deep in paper at the end of the day, of the Saturday night dances at the Empress Hotel, with Billy Tickle's orchestra playing and the rye bottles in easy reach under the tables — how exciting they had been with Aileen in her long, swishing evening dress; and yet I knew that I had to leave, and with an effort I recalled how boring life had become.

The rhythm of the railroad track, hour after hour, for four days and nights. That was the sound of Canada, the clackety clack, and the tolling of a locomotive bell or the mournful whistling of an engine far away on the lonely prairie. It was a thrill to go by train up the canyon of the

Fraser into the mountains, where one range swept past another until the Rockies were reached; then doubling back and forth and burrowing in and out, the train, with three engines straining, topped the summit of the Great Divide and began the descent to the prairies. The valleys ran north and south and so did the mother of the valleys, the Rocky Mountain Trench, which stretched into the far yonder where the blue of the earth blended with the blue of the sky.

On the prairies, a couple of boys were riding the rods; they must have been clinging to the back of the tender, for I saw them mooching around by the locomotive at one station. They were gone by the time we left Winnipeg, for there was nothing but miles and miles and miles of scrub and rock as we skirted the Great Lakes. The trans-continental trip ended in Montreal, and Shep McMurtry was at Windsor Station to meet me.

42

I hoped to catch a cattle boat to England, and Shep had some news: the earliest I could get one would be in a couple of weeks time, as it was still April and navigation had only just begun on the Saint Lawrence, but he had fixed it up with the shipping agent for me to be taken on as a cattle hand. All that had to be done now was to pay the agent his fee, which had gone up in the past year or so and was now a lousy twenty bucks; it was a goddam racket and Shep was indignant.

So, I stayed with the McMurtrys in the apartment that I knew so well on Sherbrooke Street and had time to get to know Montreal again. As far as I could see, there had been little or no change. There was the CNR's abandoned excavation, Henry's Hole,* as it was called after Sir Henry Thornton, the Canadian National's president at the time it was dug during my years at McGill. It must have been the last major construction job undertaken before the general slowdown and there was the hole still, in all its ugliness, a gaping crater in the middle of the city.

The padlock laws were new, it was true: anyone found with literature which the police considered subversive or even anti-religious, and most of the cops were god-fearing Catholics, could have his premises locked up. A number of bookstores, not all of them leftist, were padlocked. The most serious case occurred just before I got to Montreal when the apartment of the *New York Times* correspondent was searched while he was in Ottawa; there was a fine old brouhaha over that, and Premier Maurice Duplessis's Union Nationale government, the author of the padlock laws, came in for a right royal thumping from the English-speaking press outside Quebec.

What was crazy was the way that the English-speaking élite of Westmount, which had the moral and political outlook of the Cliveden set in the United Kingdom, lined up with all the greasy long-haired liberals and socialists on this issue. The fact was that the padlock laws could be used as another stick with which to beat the French Canadians, and thus they served to emphasise the split in Montreal — but there was nothing new about that. Ever since the beginning, the English-speaking and the

---

*Now the site of the Central Station, Queen Elizabeth Hotel and Place Ville Marie.

French-speaking had gone their separate ways and lived their separate lives. While I was in Montreal, I could truthfully say that I had never met a French Canadian socially, even an English-speaking French Canadian.

Despite the Duplessis government being so reactionary, there were regular shirted fascists in Quebec under their own pint-sized, French Canadian führer, Adrien Arcand. They were a mixture of hoodlums and students, and just like the spielers on the tourist buses, you couldn't tell them apart in their uniforms; they marched around and when they were allowed to, broke up leftist meetings and stoned Jewish stores. Many of the students at the University of Montreal were fascists or fascist sympathizers, and this was hardly surprising as the university was a Catholic institution engaged at the time in rallying support for Franco. I was told by one fellow that Adrien Arcand helped to launch "l'achat chez nous", the "buy French" campaign, and had distributed a list of certified French Canadian firms, but another fellow, who had been in my class in McGill, said that Arcand and his bully boys were getting a lot of credit that they didn't deserve. However, he did say that it was disgusting the way so many English Canadian firms were trying to get on this list by adding a French Canadian director to their boards.

For old times sake, we had to have a party before I sailed, but we found that we had invited so many people that we couldn't afford enough booze; we didn't know what to do until Shep suggested that we should buy some potable alcohol and make our own gin. It was a fiendishly clever scheme. We got the alcohol from the Quebec Liquor Commission and the juniper juice from the drugstore; we couldn't stop laughing as we added water and sloshed it around in a basin in the bathroom. The party was a wild success — most of the guests passed out before midnight. (Apparently, we hadn't added enough water to the alcohol, which was overproof.) We spent the next day recuperating at Como and still laughing, even though it felt as if we had dried our insides with a blow torch.

43

There were a number of other seedy looking characters beside myself sitting on the stone curb or hanging about the entrance to Shed 16 on the Montreal waterfront, where the agent said to meet him. I had on an old gray flannel shirt and a pair of dirty khaki pants which Shep had given me; he had worked his way to England on a cattle boat and knew what to wear. I had a battered old suitcase and a duffle bag. A huge wooden Christ with a halo of electric light bulbs looked down on us, and on one of the gray buildings, and gray was the colour of the day, an electric sign repeated, "Saint Joseph Protégez Nous". It was all very depressing. Across the way, freight cars were being shunted.

At noon, the agent appeared and we signed on the crew of the *SS Manchester City*; there were two papers to sign, one of them being a waiver of our wages. Aboard ship, we were billetted in a couple of triangular cabins in the forecastle, with a dozen bunks in each; the straw mattresses were hard as boards and I didn't get any sleep the first night, but after that I slept like a log.

Soon, the cattle began pouring on board from cattle cars shunted alongside the *Manchester City*; they ran through the stalls built from stem to stern on the lower deck and over most of the open upper deck, where they had been squeezed in alongside the derricks and winches. The ship had been turned into a floating barn, a goddam Noah's Ark, as Joe said — he was an unemployed kid from Toronto who was my mate. Dutch, the foreman, who looked like one of the seven dwarfs, Grumpy or Doc, called everyone Joe, but Joe was this kid's real name. The hardest cattle to handle came from Alberta, off the open range; they bucked and they barged, and they were real bastards to tie down.

"That mucking Noah had it easy," Joe said. "He had only two of them while we got seven hundred."

The food was god-awful slop. The "peggy" had to haul it from the galley, which was amidship in the clean, glistening white superstructure that housed the officers and the passengers. We soon found out that we were the lowest of the low on this class-conscious British ship; the officers would only speak when spoken to, and even the junior officers maintained their dignity by ignoring the lower orders, replying only to a direct question and then walking haughtily away. The coffee was like dishwater and I gave up drinking it. For breakfast, we had porridge without milk and fish and potatoes.

"This mucking fish wasn't caught," Joe said. "It just mucking well gave itself up."

Bad as the food was, there wasn't enough of it. One night, several of the boys in our cabin didn't get any of the oily stew that the peggy had brought up in a can, and they were ready to mutiny.

"The mucking sons of bitches, what do they think they're doing — trying to starve us!"

"This isn't the mucking Middle Ages."

"We mucking well paid to come on board. That mucking Limey captain had better watch out."

"It's a mucking racket, that's what it is — paying to be on a mucking prison ship."

The fact that each of the cattle hands had had to pay a fee to the agent of fifteen or twenty dollars, depending on how much he figured he could get out of the applicant, really rankled. However, it must be said that the fee covered a passage back as a passenger.

"Not so mucking long ago, they used to pay us for working on these tubs. Now we mucking well pay them for the privilege of these mucking prison conditions."

"It's those mucking McGill students that done this," one of the old sweats in our cabin said.

Some of those who had gone short went to the galley and were given a helping of pudding by the cook. That was the way the mutiny was settled.

It was a hard life but a healthy one, and by the time we had passed Newfoundland and were in the open Atlantic, we had become seagoing cowboys. Up at 4.30 A.M. to feed and water the cattle, and there was a right way of doing it, learned only after you had several pails of water spilled by the eagerness of the animals for a drink: "Kick them in the snout first," said Dutch, "then swing the pail into the trough." No cleaning, thank God, and the shit was knee deep by the time we got to Liverpool; if the food had been half decent, it would have been a pleasant trip — or so we thought in the warmth and exuberance of the Gulf Stream.

That was before the storm struck. The first warning was the way the sky darkened and the sea became leaden, and we realized that something ominous was going to happen when a sailor battened down our portholes. The *Manchester City* began to heave; the bow, where we were, rose and at its height when we were hanging on to the bunks, shud-

144

dered, and then plunged down to the sickening depths; there was a swish of water and a thundering crash as the ship drove into the monstrous leaden waves.

"Oh Mother Nature," groaned one of the boys in his bunk, "Mother Nature, Mother Nature." The whole crazy ark was pitching and tossing and anything loose would come banging down to add to the noise of the storm. The cattle didn't like it any more than the cattlemen, some of whom had joined the animals on the lower deck because they figured that the centre of the ship would be steadier; the cattle mooed and moaned but they didn't throw up — they couldn't, according to one of the college boys among us, because they had double stomachs.

We had a sweepstake on who was going to be sick first. I drew the second favourite, my mate Joe, who didn't let me down but vomited just a few moments before the favourite, the Mother Nature boy. The cabins were a filthy mess, and the lavatories were so foul that I had stopped using them even before the storm, but I wasn't afraid of constipation, not with the record that Captain Bligh set.

You could go down quickly. Nobody washed or cleaned up, and the fellows would lie down without taking their boots off. Nobody shaved. It was hardly surprising that a notice should be posted informing the cattlemen that the deck was no place for them to loiter.

"Why, the bloody British bastards. They mucking well don't want to see us." There was a great deal of resentment of that notice.

On the day we sighted land, the dark green hills of Ireland growing ever closer, we brought up bales of hay by crane from the hold, so that they could be ready for unloading at Birkenhead the next day. From the bottom of the hold, the wires of the derrick made a pattern against the blue sky, a pattern through which the gulls wove in and out. It was dangerous work, which we should never have done.

"They're mucking well exploiting us," one of the old soldiers said. "This is stevedore's work."

The great iron derrick hook could have smashed a man's skull like an egg shell. It was obvious that Dutch had no experience in the work; bales of hay kept falling back into the hold. One sling of five bales, which had not been landed on the deck properly, slipped and plunged down; there were cries of alarm and we scurried for the shelter of a girder, but one fellow tripped and fell. The plummetting sling with its ton of compressed hay bounced at the end of its slack, a few inches above his body. Another fellow was knocked out by a falling bale, but it was a glancing blow and he wasn't seriously hurt.

After hauling up three hundred bales of hay, we were hot and hungry, and the smells from the galley were delicious, but the steaks and roasts being cooked there were for the passengers and the officers, not for us. When we returned to the forecastle, we found the usual swill, the stringy meat that was half fat and a tasteless rice pudding. The boys were in a mutinous mood; there was talk of a sit-down strike, but it was obviously too late to do anything.

The next day, all was forgotten as we perched on the winches or leaned against the railing in the pale sunshine of the muddy Mersey and watched tweedy English cattlemen with their hefty stocks drive the steers off the ship. We chortled at the antics of the heavy animals as they pranced down the gangway, skittered on the dock, then dashed over a bridge and through a fenced runway to the Birkenhead stock yards. The poor beasts — they seemed so pleased to find their land legs again; they would be fattened up for a month on the hay and oats we had brought over, and then slaughtered to make "prime British beef".

44

As soon as I got to London, I looked up Henry Turner, the secretary of the Empire Press Union, and found him in his office, which was up one flight of stairs and at the back of an old building on Fleet Street, just across the road from the shining facades of the *Daily Telegraph* and the *Daily Express*. Through the centuries, the floor seemed to have become canted at an angle, but the office itself was bright and clean, newly painted white and comfortably carpeted. Mr. Turner, who was to become Sir Henry Turner, had on a black coat and striped pants, and a neatly rolled umbrella and a bowler hat hung from a coat rack in one corner of the room. He looked at Ken Drury's letter and grumbled about the way Canadian editors wanted him to find jobs for their men but would offer nothing in return. He had a clipped military way of speaking which gave me confidence. I planned to spend the summer travelling, and Turner said that he should be able to find me a place by the time I returned, which raised my spirits and sent me whistling down Fleet Street.

So, it was off on the grand tour which took me up the Rhine and down the Danube and across the Soviet Union. A first look at Europe, and a last look before the holocaust — already Austria had gone, swept away in the so-called Anschluss, and the Nazi tide was threatening Czechoslovakia. Boy Peter, as one of my aunts used to call me to my annoyance, Boy Peter to the dark continent had come.

In Paris, it was the anniversary of the Paris Commune of 1871, and the Popular Front was planning a big demonstration. "Tous au Mur des Féderés", *Le Populaire* cried, and more than a hundred thousand assembled in the grim cobblestone streets around the Place de la Bastille and the Cours de Vincennes to honour the "martyrs of the Commune"; it took some seven hours for this great throng to pass through the Cemetery of Père-Lachaise where the "martyrs" are buried. It was impressive all right, and a sign of the continuing strength of the Popular Front, and yet, despite the forest of red flags and the chorus of revolutionary slogans, it might have been a funeral parade. Perhaps this was due to the depressing atmosphere of the necropolis, but there was something gray and listless about the crowd, and the shouts of "Ouvrez les frontiers" (the Spanish frontiers) were hopeless. The frontiers, which had been effectively closed by the non-intervention policy, would only be opened now to allow the Spanish Loyalists to escape.

In Bonn, I stayed at the home of Dr. Rechs, a friend of an uncle of mine, on Bachstrasse; he spoke of the "yellow peril" and I found out he wasn't talking about the Japanese, as I thought, but the poor wretched Chinese, who were no threat to anyone at that time and couldn't have been as they were being slaughtered by the Japanese in establishing their East Asian Co-prosperity Sphere. A magazine cover displayed a picture of Hitler in heroic pose beside a beetle-shaped car, and Dr. Rechs explained that this was the Volkswagen, the people's car, which the Nazis were going to produce so that every German would have a car. My host was a Nazi, at least he had a swastika badge in the buttonhole of his coat lapel, but it didn't seem to be any more sinister than being a Rotarian, and aside from his beard, Dr. Rechs, who was a lawyer, might have been a Rotarian. His young partner, who also wore a Nazi badge, certainly looked like one — I was a past master at spotting Rotarians, having had to cover so many Rotary lunches in Victoria.

Up the Rhine, and I had to admit that I hadn't seen many signs of resurgent militarism. Perhaps the romantic castles got in the way! The brightest uniforms were worn by the newspaper and lottery salesmen in Munich, yellow-brown with a black swastika on red armbands, pillbox caps and flowing capes; my God, they were swish! Certainly they were better turned out than Dr. Goebbels, who stood up in the royal box in the Vienna Opera House and gave the Nazi salute.

"Heil Hitler" — it was "good day"; "Heil Hitler" — it was "hello"; and you found yourself saying it if you didn't want to be conspicuous.

You wouldn't have been able to tell Dr. Goebbels from the bigger thugs who surrounded him if he hadn't been the only one in uniform. They slurped beer during the intermission in the roccoco splendour of the Vienna (Gross Deutschland) Opera House; it was all so hellish middle class and German.

Oh, the Wachau, and Boy Peter climbed to the jagged ruins of the Castle Dürnstein, the robber baron's nest, where Richard the Lion-Heart had been imprisoned, and the peasants were inbred, but the wine was singing good.

Dr. Pissko, whom God preserve, a Czech foreign ministry official, was making arrangements for me on the telephone when he asked me what I was; I told him I was a Canadian and he immediately said I was an American, and rightly so because no one in Czechoslovakia would know what a Canadian was. On the train, a patriotic Czech said, pointing to the map of his country framed in glass behind our seat, "A small country but our own."

Up Strahov Plateau in Prague to the mighty Masaryk Stadium, where the tenth *Slet*, the Congress of Sokols (gymnasts), was being held, and two hundred and fifty thousand people watched ten thousand and more boys and girls do calisthenics to music on a field five times the size of a football field; along the steep road to the stadium, the crowds were thrilled by the sight of the latest model antiaircraft guns, stripped for action, with their crews on the alert. A British journalist told me that it was quite a sight to see the Czech defences along the Sudeten border, there were fortifications every few hundred yards and steel-helmeted troops standing guard.

Then, why didn't the Czechs fight? They had the best-equipped army in Europe and one of its greatest armament industries in the Skoda works; I saw the outside of this huge war machine when I visited Pilsen — a high wall surrounding acres of noisy buildings belching smoke. Even if the Czechs were betrayed by their friends, the British and the French, they could have fought, and who knows what would have happened, if they had. Then, why didn't they?

I was the guest of Count Aladaar von Igmandy de Boldogasszonyfa (I kept his card) at his estate at Somogynagybajom (also off the card) and went riding on the plains of Hungary. The contrast between Budapest and the country was crazy: it was like taking a journey into the past. We left the great modern city, and a most beautiful city too, and travelled by a hundred-mile-an-hour diesel train to our destination, where there was a coach and pair to meet us. Conditions in the country were simply feudal: the peasants went barefooted and if they had shoes, they carried them in their hands — I saw them doing this. The count had a young cousin who was about my age and rode miles to see me; poor guy, he probably didn't get a chance to talk politics, buried as he was in the nineteenth century, and he spoke English well, as he had been educated in the United States.

The Magyar, he said, was being nailed to Hitler's crooked cross. The Nazis were everywhere, and they had a stranglehold on the economy. He was anti-Nazi, but most of the Hungarians were pro-Nazi. There was no doubt what would happen, and the young landowner shook his head. It was all so dreadful and inevitable.

Across Rumania we travelled all night sitting up, and didn't reach the frontier station of Tighina till almost noon the next day; there, the train was reduced to the single coach occupied by myself and about a dozen other passengers. When we crossed the wooden bridge over the muddy

Dniester River, the dividing line between the two worlds at that time, the train stopped on the Rumanian side to let the Rumanian guards off, and on the Russian side to let the Russian guards on, then chugged through wheat fields for a couple of miles before coming to a halt at the first Soviet station.

Comrade Braniloff of Intourist, resplendent in a white Russian shirt, told me that this was Tiraspol and the port of entry in my passport was Odessa. (Curses, my geography was so bad that I figured the Black Sea port was on the Rumanian border when I got my Russian visa in London.) Comrade Braniloff said that he would wire Moscow to get the visa corrected. Meanwhile, I would have to stay at the station and since I was not officially in Russia, my Intourist meal tickets would not be accepted, and I would have to pay good Canadian dollars for my meals. Boy Peter was a prisoner of the Soviets. It didn't last long, just a day before authorization was received, but Comrade Braniloff, who did his best to soothe me, expressed the view that if I were a typical product of the capitalist system, there must be a lot of nervously sick people on the other side of the border.

It was with some reluctance that Intourist agreed to my going to the Hippodrome, which was on no official tour of Moscow. My interpreter-guide, a thickset fellow whose regular job was school teaching, had never been to the horse races before, and didn't know there were any. When we arrived at the gray wooden czarist relic of a Hippodrome, my guide was horrified at what he saw. There was pari-mutual betting going on. "Why," he said, "this is nothing but gambling." He was much relieved when the assistant director of the Hippodrome, a horsy looking Slav with a pair of field glasses suspended over his chest, dismissed the crowd as "a bunch of nervously sick people". The comrade assistant director was explicit, the Soviet government allowed this pari-mutual betting because it didn't want illegal gambling. My guide almost cheered when the assistant director characterised the crowd as a bunch of bigshots, engineers and so on — they were not workers!

Caviar for breakfast was what I got on the Soviet ship in which I sailed from Leningrad to London, and caviar for lunch and dinner too. I was one of the few passengers aboard, as the ship was going to be refitted. The officers and crew put on their whitest whites and stood at attention as we passed through the Kiel Canal. A troop of Hitler Jugend walked up and down, looking at the ship, and I remarked on how interested they were.

"Yes," the purser said. "They are examining a potential enemy."

45

Back in London, Henry Turner had no news. The summer was a bad time to get anything like this done, he apologised, since people were away on holidays, but he should have more success now. However, the days and the weeks went by, and he had nothing to report. This was my idea of hell. I hated hanging around waiting, keeping going on hope but always feeling the gnawing ulcer of despair. I was running out of money and I couldn't go on bumming off my uncle.

The fact was that Henry Turner had an almost impossible task, and if he hadn't been such a dedicated secretary of the Empire Press Union, who felt a responsibility for young fellows like myself, I would never have got a job on Fleet Street. First, he had to find a British reporter who wanted to go to Canada and then he had to get him a place on a Canadian paper — and that was just the beginning. One day I thought everything was arranged; Basil Dean had been found as my counterpart in the exchange and he had even booked his passage, when I was told that the matter had to be approved by the National Union of Journalists because the *Daily Herald*, which was the paper involved, had a closed shop with the union. So, there was a further delay. Meanwhile, the Munich crisis was deepening. War might end our little exchange.

A tall bespectacled youth, Basil Dean,* whose fair hair was neatly parted and plastered down, was a junior reporter on the *Daily Herald* and acted as a researcher and leg man for Hannen Swaffer. We got along well together and we had a lot in common, because he was an ardent socialist and so was I.

Through him, I met Hannen Swaffer, the great journalist, the "pope of Fleet Street", who was writing a column for the *Daily Herald* then. He looked like an Edwardian actor in his turn-of-the-century dark blue suit, high collar and cravat, and yet he didn't look out of place striding through the Covent Garden market, with its ripe stench of vegetables, to his apartment on the fourth floor of a building opposite the Nurse Cavell memorial above Trafalgar Square. He was from Kent: "I'm the l-l-last of the Englishmen," he said, with his rich, ripe stammer, and he had a

*In the exchange, Dean went to the Hamilton *Spectator*; he stayed in Canada and when he died in 1968 was publisher of the *Edmonton Journal*.

bulbous John Bull nose above his thin lips, which were tobacco stained from the cigarette that hung smouldering and dripping ashes, even when he talked. He was a left-wing socialist, yet he was also the leading spiritualist in Britain, since the death of Sir Oliver Lodge.

When the exchange was finally arranged, and Basil was leaving in a couple of days time and I was to begin work the following Monday, Swaff did us the signal honour of inviting us to lunch at the Savoy Hotel. He had a special table there on one side of the dining room, where he held court, and we sat on either side of him, with his secretary, who sat opposite him, looking like a princess who had been turned into a frog.

"S-S-Sir Samuel and L-L-Lady Hoare," the great journalist said scornfully and loud enough so that all the attentive diners could hear. "I've heard of a whore marrying to become a lady, but this is the f-f-first time a lady married to become a Hoare."

"Ha, ha." It was an old chestnut, but we laughed and our laughter was echoed at other tables.

Among those who came over to greet Swaff and consult him was a tall, distinguished looking man, Sir William Jowitt, attorney general in the former Labour government. It was the last days of the Munich crisis, and Jowitt was worried: some of the government departments had already been moved out of London; the Home Office was in Wormwood Scrubs prison, which was the right place for it, he said with a chuckle. There was nothing to be alarmed about at that, since bureaucracy easily frightened, but he had been reliably informed that the orders for general mobilization had been drawn up and would be issued in a day or two.

"What are you going to do if there is a war, Swaff?" Jowitt asked.

"I'll do just what I d-d-did in the l-l-last war," the great journalist said; "n-n-nothing."

A ripple of excited comment travelled across the Savoy dining room.

"The odds are on war," a businessman told Swaff; he had consulted his bookmaker and it was "two to one for".

At the approach of Armageddon, the unemployed, who had been left hanging around doing nothing for a whole decade, were put to work digging trenches in the park.

"They're digging their own g-g-graves," Hannen Swaffer said, and soon a grateful country, which had no use for them in peacetime, would call them up in wartime.

It was pathetic, this scrabbling around, and at night too, under flood-lights — the grass would be ruined. They were piling sandbags by the ground floor windows of the government buildings on Whitehall, and unlimbering antiaircraft guns; I counted three of them around Westminster Abbey and the Houses of Parliament. Later, the papers, including the *Daily Herald*, were to claim that one of these ack ack guns was of 1916 vintage and hadn't been fired since the war. Then, the government began shovelling out gas masks to anyone and everyone, including even visitors like myself, and that really scared the hell out of the British.

The tension had reached the breaking point by the time Prime Minister Chamberlain went to Munich — and on his return, there was genuine, if somewhat shamefaced relief; I was walking toward Piccadilly Circus when the newsboys began shouting "peace in our time", and the dull gray crowds suddenly became alive and joyful. There was laughter again on the streets of London.

46

Shortly after I joined the *Daily Herald* I climbed the side of a ship at dead of night to tell the British Legion men aboard that there was to be no plebiscite in Czechoslovakia and that their trip was off. The recruitment of these veterans was one of the dirtiest deceptions of the whole lousy Munich crisis: it was a result of the Runciman Mission to Czechoslovakia, whose real purpose was to prepare British public opinion for the sellout of the Sudetenland to Hitler. At no time did Lord Runciman give a hoot for a plebiscite, he considered it a useless undertaking, a "sheer formality", but the Chamberlain government had to have something to cover up the dismemberment and destruction of a democracy.

So, the old soldiers were taken on to police a plebiscite-that-was-not-to-be and their recruitment and "embarcation" in two liners were given maximum publicity. The deception could not be maintained for long, and finally the government had to announce that there would be no vote. By then the veterans must have smelled a rat, for their ships had been anchored off Southend Pier for days. Most of them were in their bunks when I climbed aboard and went from cabin to cabin, spreading the news; the old sweats grumbled and cursed, but only halfheartedly, for they had suspected the worst. I wrote my story and telephoned it from the lighthouse at the end of Southend Pier and earned my first by-line on the *Daily Herald*.

On another assignment, I was sent to Newhaven to meet the Spanish Loyalist refugees who had been given a temporary asylum in Great Britain. Among them were Colonel Casado, who handed over Madrid and central Spain to Franco; General Menendez, who headed the Spanish Republican Army of the Levant, and one of his corps commanders, Colonel Gustavo Duran. As the boat train rushed through the English countryside glistening green in the afternoon sunshine, Colonel Duran, who spoke English and was fair haired and didn't look like a Spaniard (he was a Catalan), talked about the chaos of the last few days. While making his way to the coast, he had been caught by the fascists but escaped; however, he had seen Valencia in Franco's hands — there were Moors everywhere, he said, and on guard at every building, which just showed how much the Caudillo trusted his own people.

The Colonel had been a musical composer in Madrid before the civil war. What was he going to do? He didn't know.

"You are from Canada," Colonel Duran said. "Is there any chance of my going there?"

There were sequels to both these stories. On the day after Hitler took over the rest of truncated Czechoslovakia, and the Nazis marched into Prague, I was sent to the Czech legation; only a few weeks before I had been at the Spanish embassy to witness the last rites of the republicans, as the British government had just recognized Franco. While we were at the Czech legation awaiting developments, since nobody seemed to know what was going to happen, a little man who was probably a clerk staggered past us, his arms laden down with files and papers; the photographers gave chase, but after dodging back and forth, he was able to elude them. A few minutes later, a harassed Czech official came over to me and asked if I were a photographer; I said no, but there they were over there.

"You tried to take pictures of that man," the official said to them. "You must not. Don't you know the Gestapo will get them. Some of us must go back to Czechoslovakia."

The continuing crisis, the daily scare headlines, were beginning to have their effect, even on the phlegmatic British, and there were crisis dreams duly reported in the papers, together with their interpretations by psychiatrists, or "trick cyclists" as they were called in British army slang. There was one about appearing before Hitler in one's pyjamas which was interpreted to mean that one was ashamed of being afraid of the man.

At a party in Henry Turner's eighteenth century house in Hampstead, one of the guests told how he almost started a riot by suggesting that Hitler might be right. Mrs. Turner was E. Arnot Robertson the novelist, a witty and original woman. She had got an artist friend to decorate her dining room walls with cave drawings, and the simple line drawings of the prehistoric hunt were in striking contrast to her Regency furniture. The guest, who was a Fabian socialist and was considering running for the Labour Party in the next election, said that he thought it was about time someone took an opposite stand. So, when he was in his pub one night and there was the usual moaning and groaning about the Nazis, this chap got up and asked if anyone didn't think that Hitler might be right, that the Germans should be united as one people.

Well, he said, as we sipped liqueurs after dinner, there was silence in the pub, aghast silence, then someone, and he wasn't able to identify him, shouted: "You're nothing but a traitor." The half-dozen people at the Turner's party chuckled, but I wondered whether he had been simply voicing his true feelings. There were many sincere pacifists in the Labour Party who regarded Hitler as a lesser evil than war.

After Prague, though, there was not much doubt that war was inevitable, and even the *Daily Express* stopped printing front page assurance that there would be no war this year nor next year either.

It was a grim time. Chamberlain had been betrayed. He was a broken man; he sat crumpled on the treasury bench in the House of Commons on the day Hitler rode into Prague. Hannen Swaffer looked like a judge from a Victorian melodrama; his thin lips, stained with nicotine, shook, and he flicked ash off his smouldering cigarette onto his blue suit as he began to stammer out a thought.

"You could t-t-trust the bloody Tories always to do everything wrong," he said. They were going to make a stand over Poland now, and Poland was just as indefensible as far as the British were concerned as Czechoslovakia, "that faraway c-c-country about whose p-p-people we know so little", and Swaff mimicked Chamberlain's sepulchral tones.

"It'll be the s-s-supreme bloody irony," he went on, "to go to war over Poland, an out-and-out d-d-dictatorship, when we wouldn't fight for a democracy like Czechoslovakia, and in f-f-fact, were instrumental in destroying it. And m-m-mark my word, there's g-g-going to be no getting out of this treaty."

47

As an exchange reporter on the *Daily Herald*, I received the NUJ (National Union of Journalists) minimum for Fleet Street, which was nine guineas a week; it was more than twice as much as the $22.50 a week that I was getting when I left the *Victoria Daily Times*. Besides this salary, there were expenses: I forget what day we made out our weekly expense account, but when I came to do my first one, the reporter who had the desk next to mine, a bushy-moustached fellow named A. J. McWhinney, announced that he would make mine out for me — and McWhinney proceeded to do so, stopping my protests that I hadn't spent anything like that amount by fixing me sternly with his glasses, which magnified his eyes, and saying that I should regard it as a minimum, otherwise I would be letting the side down. The swindle sheets were an in-joke that was always being told on Fleet Street, and there was the story of a *Daily Express* reporter who charged for a taxi upstairs! What astonished me was that management accepted these swindle sheets without demur; I suppose they were regarded as a lesser evil than raises.

Francis Williams was the editor, a round Falstaffian figure, just as fat as Ritchie Calder, the science reporter, was thin; Stephen Taylor* was the medical correspondent, and Charlie Leatherland, who looked like and was a countryman, the assistant news editor — all of them were to be made peers, the life Lords who would take over the moribund British upper house. Leatherland, who had a stentorian voice and was known as Leatherlungs, would shout across the news room, "Stursberg, I wish to have intercourse with you", which was a quite proper, if unusual, use of English.

It was a tremendous thrill, after the small town *Victoria Daily Times*, to be on a paper with a circulation of two million a day. (The *Daily Herald* was the first to reach that figure, although by 1938 the *Daily Express* had surpassed it.) Of the great nationals, the *Daily Herald* was the only one to have the all-inclusive American-style news room, and this was said to be due to the fact that one of the few movies that Lord Southwood, the publisher and head of Odhams Press, had seen was

*Rt. Hon. Lord Taylor of Harlow, Chancellor of Memorial University, New-foundland, who helped settle the Saskatchewan doctors' strike.

Front Page. The great horseshoe-shaped sub editors' desk dominated the news room, and I was to find that a popular paper of this magnitude was closely edited. (There had been little editing on the *Times* and no rewriting.)

At the head of the horseshoe-shaped table sat the chief sub editor, and beside him the "copy taster" who did just that — he looked at the copy, threw away the crap, put a notation on a story if he thought it worth using, and passed it on to the chief sub; if the chief sub agreed, he would decide on its length, heading, and what page it would go, and he would pass it to the page sub who would rewrite it. The rewriting was such that reporters hardly recognized their own stories, and in fact, there were celebrations in the local pubs when more than a sentence of the original copy survived.

"They're mine, old boy, those beautiful words — I wrote them, all ten of them."

When I first joined the *Daily Herald*, in my enthusiasm and innocence, I asked the news services editor, who was my immediate boss, if he would like me to write something about Canada; I wasn't very specific, I admit, but the offer didn't appeal to L. M. MacBride, who, like Hannen Swaffer, had a stammer.

"Stursberg," he said, "th-th-there's one thing you'll have to learn. We n-n-never have anything about Canada in this paper because n-n-nothing ever happens there. You've got no g-g-gangsters, no Hollywood — you're a d-d-dull country."

Hannen Swaffer was equally scathing when I interviewed him in the comfortable drawing room of his flat, where Sir Henry Segrave* had appeared during a seance, or so Swaff told me, and where there was a spirit painting of the great journalist, a ghostly figure behind his own portrait, which looked remarkably like himself.

"Canada," Swaff said, "has n-n-no art, no literature, no theatre, or n-n-none that I have ever heard of, but th-th-then you're a new country, you have vigour and vitality and the g-g-great open spaces to conquer, while c-c-culture is a result of decay. When you look at a ruin and say how b-b-beautiful, you're not admiring the red brick in all its h-h-horror, you're admiring the m-m-moss and the lichen; in the end, you're admiring the worms."

Some time later, in the spring of 1939, I was called into the office of the feature editor, who was a huge man, at least six feet five inches and God knows how many "stones", named Tom Darlow. The managing

*Famous British racing driver and popular hero who was the first man to travel at more than 200 mph on land. He was killed on June 13, 1930 attempting to break his own world record of 231.446 mph, set the previous year.

editor of the *Daily Herald* then was Percy Cudlip, who was to succeed Francis Williams as editor.

"Stursberg," Tom Darlow said, "the King and Queen are going to Canada, and we shall need an editorial page article from you. What can you do?"

I was delighted and said that I could describe the main places where the King and Queen would go.

"No, no, no," the feature editor said. "The movies will do that much better than you can. Do me a piece about a half a dozen prominent Canadians the King and Queen will meet."

"Yessir," I said, but it was really accepting under false pretences because I didn't know who the six leading Canadians were or anything about them. What the hell, my total journalistic experience was a few years in Victoria, which was really off the Canadian map, but I wasn't going to miss this chance to write an article on the editorial page of the *Daily Herald*; I was determined to do it even if the subject were beyond me. I racked my brains and recalled that there was a famous Canadian journalist in London, J. B., "Hamish", McGeachy, the correspondent of the *Winnipeg Free Press*. As a junior reporter on the *Victoria Times*, I had read and admired the syndicated column he had written, under the by-line "J.B.M.", on the Rowell Sirois Commission's meetings.

After a lot of telephoning around, I got hold of him, and we met in the basement of the Falstaff, a pub on Fleet Street. When I apologised for picking his brains in this blatant manner, Hamish, who looked like a pirate, a Captain Morgan reincarnated, with a Scots accent somewhat muffled by cigarettes and whisky, said that he was delighted to be of service and that he found that he hadn't much to do in London, in any case. The *Free Press* didn't seem to want much. It was all too easy for him, and paying due regard to regional representation, he rattled off the names of six leading Canadians, along with a few juicy details about each, while I scribbled notes. In fact, he practically dictated my editorial page piece.

Who were the six prominent Canadians whom the King and Queen would meet? Of course, Prime Minister William Lyon Mackenzie King had to head the list; he was dull all right, the sort of leader that the British would have expected. The others were Premier Maurice Duplessis of Quebec and Premier Mitch Hepburn of Ontario, who were not dull, nor was Bible Bill Aberhart, the prophet of Social Credit and premier of Alberta, and Dr. Allan Roy Dafoe, the country doctor who had delivered the Dionne quintuplets, and lastly, Dr. Lyle Telford, the socialist mayor of Vancouver, and the only one I knew anything about.

Before going on any further, I should set the record straight and say that any piece for the editorial page was not subject to the brutal editing of a news story and was never rewritten. After this article appeared — and I recall that its publication was the greatest triumph of my young life up to then (the by-line was one of the biggest I have ever received) — Tom Darlow called me in again and said that since the King and Queen were still in Canada, the paper would want another two editorial page articles on Canada, and to give him some ideas as to subject matter.

I did and as I expected, he chose "The Indians" and "The Great North", both of which conformed with the popular view of Canada as a land of wide open spaces, of Indians and Eskimos and Mounties, and which more or less endorsed Swaffer's theory that it was a country without culture because it was a new country. When these articles were published, I returned to the news services editor, who had been so scornful when I had suggested writing something about Canada, and said to him:

"Well, we didn't do so badly by Canada, did we?"

"Yes, old b-b-boy," MacBride said, "I've been reading your editorial page p-p-pieces. But quite frankly, old boy, there won't be another th-th-thing about Canada in the paper for the next nine years."

48

Of all the pubs around the *Daily Herald*, the Freemason's Arms was the most undistinguished, with a decor that was brewery baronial of a very recent period, and yet it had some claim to fame, as it opened at five o'clock in the morning for the benefit of the costermongers and workers in the Covent Garden market. The *Daily Herald's* offices were just around the corner from the market and the opera house in Longacre and when I was on the late night shift, from 8.30 P.M. to 4.30 A.M., we used to play cards in the news room till the Freemason's opened, and then drink with the cockney barrow boys and the porters. We would drink whisky and milk until the sun was up and I would take the underground home while everyone else was coming to work. I had a bedsitting room at 28 Trebovir Road, Earl's Court, and I used to take the Piccadilly line train. On more than one occasion, I fell asleep and was carried out to the end of the line, above ground in what seemed the country, where I was wakened up and put on a return train.

The boardinghouse where I stayed was a home away from home, as a number of Victorians lived there, including Denny Diespecker and Doreen Swayne, who was the daughter of the editor of the Victoria *Daily Colonist*. It was Denny who told me about 28 Trebovir Road — I used to see him in the upstairs lounge and reading room of British Columbia House, Regent Street, which was a great place to hang out if you had nothing to do.

Although most pubs in London closed at 11 P.M. — I was to find that in certain parts of the country, they closed at 10 P.M. and some as early as 9.30 P.M. — it was said that you could, if you persevered and were willing to travel far enough, drink at any time of the day or night in a London pub. The Freemason's Arms was one of the calls if you wanted to go on an all-night pub crawl, which I didn't attempt; others which opened at peculiar hours were in Billingsgate or Smithfield or other market areas. There were all-night drinking clubs, but they were more expensive: draught beer was four pence halfpenny a half pint in the saloon bar, four pence in the private bar, and three pence halfpenny in the public bar. The class distinctions in the pubs (the saloon bar was for businessmen and professional people, the private bar for the tradesmen and the servants, and the public bar for the workers) were beginning to disappear at the end of the thirties.

I remember one pub crawl in which we visited Dirty Dick's, taking the underground to the ugly, smokey barn of Liverpool Street Station and then down dark streets to Cheapside; it was an old pub and had once been called the Gates of Jerusalem, since it was just outside the old Jewish quarter of the city, but now it was famous for its dirt — it claimed to be the dirtiest pub in London. The walls and ceilings were decorated with the macabre remains of dried animals, and these were gray, hideous, dusty and festooned with cobwebs, as they hadn't been cleaned since they were put up, and nobody knew when that was. It was a nightmare pub, and the *Daily Herald* crowd with whom I was making this pub crawl said that, as a newcomer, I had the right to stroke the dead cat on the wall and make a wish. When I demurred, the barman whose white shirt and apron shone immaculately against the background of dirt and decay, joined in the attempts to persuade me.

"Gertcha," he said. "It's lucky. Corblimey, ain't you ever heard of the sacred Egyptian cat? Well, that's him — yes sir, you'll get your wish."

So, I gave in. I knew I was being had, but I didn't know how badly, for as I reached to stroke the mummified pussy, one of its dry legs kicked at me. I gasped and started away, and the whole pub shook with laughter.

49

On the day of my departure from London (instead of six months, I had been able to string out my exchange job on the *Daily Herald* to nearly nine months), a gas warfare drill was being conducted in front of the boat train platform at Waterloo Station: several men in yellow overalls, with goggle-eyed black gas masks, used a special apparatus like a tank car to spray chemicals on an area that was supposed to have been contaminated with mustard gas; then, they splashed around in pink rubber boots, swabbing up the mess. The demonstration had the effect of scaring the living bejesus out of the tourists, who chattered about the war coming and how glad they were to be going back to God's country. A man with a shining purple face which seemed to be swathed in bandages gave me a start on the train. Who the hell was he? A mustard gas victim? Later, aboard the *Ile de France*, I heard that he was the tatooed man, who was going to New York to appear in Ripley's "Believe It or Not" Odditorium.

There were no anti-gas precautions being taken in the United States, no war scare whatsoever; in fact, quite the contrary, there was a concerted effort to make out that it was business as usual. I watched Bill "Bojangles" Robinson, the great negro entertainer, celebrate his seventieth birthday in the sweltering sunshine of New York by tap-dancing down Broadway. John Steinbeck's *Grapes of Wrath* was all the rage and there was a vicarious thrill in reading about the Okies and the depression; and Erskine Caldwell's *Tobacco Road* was setting records in the theatres.

However, there were repercussions of the war crisis on the steaming hot Flushing Meadows, the World's Fair site, where the Nazis had been given the bum's rush for discriminating against Jews in the construction of their exhibit. This left the Soviet Union with the biggest, brassiest and most bejewelled building — it had a map of Russia in jewels. Yet, despite the foreign competition, the greatest crowds were outside the Futurama which Norman Bel Geddes had designed for General Motors — and there was the diorama of New York City. (This was the beginning of a craze in ramas that reached its zenith with a Christorama between Quebec City and the shrine of Ste. Anne de Beaupré.) The diorama was a cross section of New York, skyscrapers down to subway, which moved through a day in half an hour or so, while a golden radio voice declaimed a poem especially written for the show:

> This is the City of Light,
> Where Night never comes . . .

There was a great line-up of people before the Futurama, waiting for hours in the broiling sun to be taken on a simulated flight across the United States of the future. An endless belt of armchairs, like the seats in a plane, carried the visitors past models showing the great divided highways which would span the continent by 1960; loud-speakers in the backs of the chairs, fully synchronised for each individual, explained what one saw, the great divided highway climbing the mountain, with one lane sometimes above the other or wandering off quite far from the other, and encircling the great metropolises and their satellite cities.

"Boy, ain't those highways something," the old man said to his wife as they came to the end of their flight into the future, "but they're a long way off."

That was a fair assessment of the situation in Canada: the only thing that linked Vancouver to the rest of the country was the railway line, the long steel tracks of the Canadian Pacific and Canadian National railways — there was no road, and some said that none would be built through the Rockies, that it wouldn't be worth it. While the two railways took separate routes across continental Canada and different passes through the Rockies, there was only one way of getting to Vancouver from the East — through the Fraser Canyon — and both railways came down this narrow gorge, clinging to its rocky edges and crisscrossing each other as if desperately searching for the safer side. A couple of well-placed bombs could cut off Vancouver and the Pacific Coast from Canada but not from the United States, which was a comforting thought; however, no Japanese plane could fly that far, the Pacific was too big a ditch, thank God.

50

Victoria was just the same, and yet it was different. It was great to see the old pals again, Jack Trace and Gilroy and George Cameron, and the girls, although Aileen was still away, and my brother had been transferred, first up-island and then to Vancouver — but that wasn't the difference. I had lost touch in the year and a half I had been away, and the things that seemed to have been so fascinating in retrospect in London, were not now; the gossip that used to intrigue us so much in the old days had no meaning — so what if someone were going out with someone else, who cared? Yesterday, why yesterday was among the past ten thousand years!

There was no going back, no returning to the *Victoria Daily Times*, and I was to start work on the Vancouver *Province* on the day after Labour Day. Bruce Hutchison had helped me to get the job. He was now with the Vancouver *Sun* and was spending some time in the East, which meant Ottawa. He gave me some advice in a letter: "Watch your writing. In the end that counts for more than initiative, experience and brains." So, this was just a visit home to see my mother and father before moving to Vancouver; I had left Victoria the year before.

While I was away, the *Victoria Daily Times* seemed to have changed its style. Instead of the regular eight column streamer for the main story, whether it was about the result of a city council meeting or the outbreak of the Spanish Civil War, there were one or two column heads. All of which had a calming effect. The news at the end of August, 1939 called for screaming headlines in the blackest, biggest type, yet the Nazi-Soviet pact, for Christ's sake, rated a one column heading in the *Times*. Old Bill Henderson must be slipping; surely to God, he realized the significance of this sinister treaty; he looked much the same, if a little bit wispier, a little more quizzical, as he listened to my experiences.

Archie Wills was still alderman, still the same conscientious guy who didn't smoke or drink, and he got me to speak to the Monday luncheon meeting of his Gyro Club. (The next day, the *Colonist* had me saying that Europe was torn between the forces of communism and fascism while the *Times* reported that I told the Gyros that religion was a dead issue in Russia.) The editor's office had the same cheap furniture, the same slag heaps of yellowing paper as in the days of Benny Nicholas, and if anything, Ken Drury was more untidy; Ken had a habit of doing two things at once, which may have been a nervous tic, and he edited copy while talking to me. Les Fox was his bouncing self and the first to take me out for a drink. Nothing much had changed, except the make-up of the front page: the news room was the same pigsty, knee deep in paper after the last deadline, and Joe the janitor still shook his head and muttered, "Corblimey, what a mess", before cleaning up.

Outside the *Times* building, the crowd grew as the news became more and more ominous, overflowing the sidewalk into the middle of Broad Street. The hand-printed bulletins which were hung in the ground floor windows were underlined in red:

BRITISH PARLIAMENT CALLED INTO EMERGENCY SESSION

At lunch time, some of the younger office workers, stenographers and clerks from the Pemberton Building, joined the crowd, but mostly it was made up of older Victorians, the lotus eaters who had taken time off from their gardening or fishing, the retired Indian burra sahibs, the old China hands, the Bengal lancers without lances, the former tea growers of Assam and the oil wallahs of Sumatra, and the rest of those who had given up the white man's burden and come to Vancouver Island.

ZERO HOUR MAY BE TONIGHT
AFTER NAZI ULTIMATUM TO POLAND

There they stood in their tweeds and raincoats, with umbrellas and walking sticks firmly grasped in their right hands; they were not down-hearted as they had been during the dreadful time of the abdication; they were ready to stand up to Hitler, they were prepared to muddle through.

HOLIDAY CRUISES CANCELLED. LONDON BEING EVACUATED.

In the front ranks were a couple of clergymen who kept shaking their heads; their dog collars reminded me that they were ex-missionaries among the lotus eaters — and generally, they were a sad and sorry lot, especially the China missionaries, who, according to my father, were remarkable for their long faces — but the ex-missionaries were out-numbered by the former traders, the merchant adventurers, who made Shanghai a modern metropolis with skyscrapers and the longest bar in the world and built hotels like Raffles in Singapore and Flashman's in Rawalpindi and Shepherd's in Cairo:

EUROPE SHROUDED IN CENSORSHIP
BRITISH NAVY MOBILISED

Above the honking of the cars pushing through the crowd that flooded the juncture of Broad Street and Fort Street, an excited voice could be heard saying, "Mustn't miss Kaltenborn tonight".

51

It was like old times, the Saturday night dance at the Empress Hotel, only the date was September 2, 1939. Almost everyone I knew seemed to be there, including my friend Jimmy Nesbitt, the social lion on the *Times* staff. In looking back, I remember the dance and not the dancers; and except for George Cameron and the girl I was with, I can't be sure who was at our table. George arranged the party, which was a kind of farewell to me, as I was leaving for Vancouver after the holiday weekend. There was the usual Beaux Arts crowd at a long table next to us. Perhaps because of a greater awareness on that fateful night, the ballroom glittered, and the girls never looked more beautiful in their long evening gowns.

Nobody said very much about the war news: the Nazis had already driven deep into Poland, and the British and the French had done nothing yet — at least, the *Victoria Times* put an eight-column headline on *that* story, but it was in the newfangled light type that didn't make anything like the impression the old black banner lines did. George Cameron wanted to know if there were a chance of Chamberlain ratting again. I said I wouldn't bet on it, but that we should know soon because he was going to be speaking on the radio early Sunday morning and the CBC would be carrying it.

"You're coming back to my place to hear him," George said as he poured me a slug of rye; as usual, the bottles were stashed under the table in easy reach; he raised his voice so the others in the company could hear the invitation, "You're all coming around to my place after the dance."

Billy Tickle's orchestra struck up the "Beer Barrel Polka", which was at the top of the hit parade then: "Roll out the barrel, we'll have a barrel of fun," the words meant nothing, and anyone could sing the song, and soon everyone was, and the dance floor rocked and the ballroom reverberated to this Czech drinking song. It was the last thing to come out of Czechoslovakia before it was engulfed by the Nazis, or so it was said. "Roll out the barrel . . . zing boom ta rarrel", what a hell of a swansong for democracy!

At George Cameron's place we seemed to have picked up others of the old gang who weren't at our table in the Empress, including Brian Burdon-Murphy — you couldn't forget his black eyebrows — and Jack Trace.* The first thing we did was to turn on the big console radio; a dance band was playing, its music "coming from" some room in some hotel in San Francisco; it was succeeded by another dance band in another room in another hotel in San Francisco. At two o'clock, everyone stopped dancing or fooling around, and there was that moment of silence on the radio as switches were thrown and antennae reached out for the overseas transmission. "And now we bring you London," and there was Chamberlain speaking, and his lugubrious voice came through clear and static-less:

"This morning, the British ambassador in Berlin handed to the German government a final note stating that unless we heard from them by eleven o'clock that they were preparing at once to withdraw their troops from Poland, a state of war would exist between us." He spoke slowly, and it was the voice of an old man, tired and beaten. "I have to tell you that no such undertaking has been received and, in consequence, this country is at war with Germany."

There was a gasp which was almost a sob from one of the girls, and someone said, "So this is it"; but no one paid attention; everyone was straining to listen to the disembodied voice of Prime Minister Chamberlain speaking of what a "bitter blow" it had been for him that all his efforts at peace had failed. He had hoped, evidently, for an eleventh-hour Munich type agreement because, he said, "up to the very last, it would have been possible to arrange a peaceful and honourable settlement", but Hitler would have none of it, and so he had come to the conclusion that the Führer wanted war and could only be stopped by force — and this he intoned sadly, solemnly, but without conviction. Chamberlain's whole manner was that of a prison padre trying to comfort a condemned man on his way to the gallows.

It was ghastly, and as this dismal dirge went on the one babe who looked as solid as the Venus de Milo broke down and became hysterical, while the guys stared glumly ahead. Britain was going to the aid of Poland, brave Poland, Prime Minister Chamberlain said, but didn't explain how; he had received assurances of support from the Empire, which was putting the finger on us, sitting in George Cameron's room, all dolled up in our tuxes. He ended by saying:

"Now may God bless you all and may he defend the right, for it is evil things that we shall be fighting against — force, bad faith, injustice, oppression and persecution. Against them, I am certain that right will

*Both killed in the war.

prevail." It was the last liturgy, the croak of doom on a September morning.

"Son of a bitch," and it was said with such fury that it sounded like a whiplash. "They're not going to get me to fight their goddam war — they're going to have to catch me first."

"Oh yeah! Wait till they turn on the propaganda. You'll get so fired up about this war against fascism and oppression, you'll volunteer."

"One thing is certain. There won't be conscription, not after what happened in Quebec during the last war, and not by a Liberal government."

"Thank God for that mealy-mouthed bastard, Mackenzie King."

Venus de Milo seemed to have got over her hysterics and was curled up in an armchair with her head half-hidden in a pillow, sobbing softly. George Cameron was making a frantic search of the bookshelves that covered one wall of his room; he looked half-crazy with the light glinting on his thick glasses as he pulled out handfuls of books. Meanwhile, the other fellows, including myself, were gathered around the radio, which had been turned off, and were arguing about what we would do in wartime:

"You know, this is an opportunity to make a pisspot full of money. Look at the people who made fortunes out of the last war."

"Christ knows how many millionaires."

"How do you become a war profiteer?"

"It's easy. There are going to be shortages of every lousy thing, and all you have to do is to hoard."

George had found the book he was looking for and after flipping curiously through the pages, he began to recite:

> 'Twas brillig, and the slithy toves
> Did gyre and gimble in the wabe:
> All mimsy were the borogoves,
> And the mome raths outgrabe.

Everyone had stopped talking and was listening, and there were delighted murmurs as he went on in the sombre tones that Chamberlain had used:

> "Beware the Jabberwock, my son!
> The jaws that bite, the claws that catch!
> Beware the Jubjub bird, and shun
> The frumious Bandersnatch!"